WORK OF
THE
**PASTORAL
RELATIONS
COMMITTEE**

Other Judson Press books of interest

WORK OF
THE
PASTORAL
RELATIONS
COMMITTEE

Emmett V. Johnson

Judson Press® Valley Forge

WORK OF THE PASTORAL RELATIONS COMMITTEE
Copyright © 1983
Judson Press, Valley Forge, PA 19481
Third Printing, 1991

Unless otherwise indicated, Bible quotations in this volume are from the Revised Standard Version of the Bible copyrighted 1946, 1952 © 1971, 1973 by the Division of Christian Education of the National Council of the Churches of Christ in the U.S.A., and used by permission.
Other versions used in this book:
The New English Bible (NEB). Copyright © The Delegates of the Oxford University Press and The Syndics of the Cambridge University Press, 1961, 1970.

Library of Congress Cataloging in Publication Data

Johnson, Emmett V.
   Work of the pastoral relations committee.

   Bibliography: p.
   1. Pastoral relations committees—Handbooks, manuals, etc. I. Title.
BV664.J63 1983   254   83-153
ISBN 0-8170-0984-1

The name JUDSON PRESS is registered as a trademark in the U.S. Patent Office.
Printed in the U.S.A.

Contents

Preface

This book is written for laypersons who love their church and are concerned very deeply for its ministry. A basic premise is that pastors should be viewed as God's gifts to the church and, as God's gifts, should be cared for.

In ten years of service as Executive Minister of the Minnesota Baptist Conference, my heaviest and most frustrating work was mediating conflicts between pastors and congregations. I am convinced that most of the conflicts did not need to occur. How many times I have said, "If *only* there had been a covenant of expectations by both sides *and* a recognized forum for dealing with problems!"

It is my firm opinion that such a covenant and such a forum are possible within the church pastoral relations committee. The committee is not magic, nor does it function automatically. A successful committee demands hard work and must be fully and broadly owned by the congregation. But building and maintaining good relations between pastor and people—relations which, if lacking, cut the nerve of any church's effectiveness—has true potential in this committee. The potential for the demonic is also real. The wrong people on the committee, overzealously making the committee more than it is, can cause all kinds of mischief.

This book is written for pastors and committee members, but lay leaders, concerned about an effective church, can also benefit from reading it.

The book also serves another function. It becomes a basic handbook for a pastoral search committee; the fifth chapter, the largest, is given over to the whole enterprise of finding a pastor. The entire book, however, is of value to the pastoral search committee and its process because the book lifts up the issues of which that committee must be fully aware. This is why the need to have the pastoral relations committee as the core of the pastoral search committee is argued for with some forcefulness.

Although I am a Baptist and write from that point of view, the book is valuable and applicable for all groups with a free-church polity.

Establishing a Pastoral Relations Committee   1

The Christian church, among world religions, maintains a unique relationship between its professional leaders and the church members. It is spoken of as "pastor and people."

No church will fulfill its role in evangelism, nurture, education, worship, and social concern if the relationship between pastor and people is not healthy. In an era of great concern for church growth, this relationship needs to be noted carefully.

A lot of good advice is provided in seminary classes in practical theology on how that relationship operates, with a lot of attention given to the pastoral role. But who teaches the church about that relationship and how to maintain its health? Who in the church is charged with an understanding of the role of those on either side of the relationship? Who is expected to be sensitive to the unique needs and functions of the pastor? Who is the pastor's ombudsman in conflict situations?

Some group must assume this task and work at it with as much energy as the building committee puts into plans for new construction. That group is the *pastoral relations committee*. Just as the whole congregation cannot function as a committee-of-the-whole for finance or education or missions, so a small committee must be charged to act in that special field of church and pastoral relations.

At the onset the church must have a theology for ministry that gives full place to the unique contributions of both pastor and people.

Theology for Ministry

There is no *essential* difference between pastors and lay persons either in terms of their standing before God or in terms of their ministry in Jesus' name. All believers are part of a *general priesthood*. All have the right to go directly to God and are competent to lead in worship, offering "spiritual sacrifices acceptable to God" (1 Peter 2:5). All are called (and are accountable) to "declare the wonderful deeds of him who called you out of darkness into his marvelous light" (1 Peter 2:9). Marcus Barth says that the baptismal passage—"For as many of you as were baptized into Christ have put on Christ" (Galatians 3:27)—is a kind of ordination image of participating in the public ministry of Christ together with the believers. This understanding hallows the work of Christians who are mechanics, lawyers, homemakers, doctors, secretaries, and carpenters. "Whatever you do, in word or deed, do everything in the name of the Lord Jesus" (Colossians 3:17).

Within the general call to all Christians to be Christ's disciples in their vocations, there is a special call to *ministry*. That term refers to a specific order among the people of God. George Peck says that there are six factors involved in a response to that specific call to ministry:

1. The presence of particular gifts;
2. The presence of particular occasions for their use;
3. Preparation for the use of these gifts (usually includes education);
4. Recognition of the particular call by others who are competent, especially recognition by the church;
5. Commissioning and appointing by the church;
6. Support and accountability.

Some will exercise that special calling to *minister* outside of the church in the secular world. Generally these are laity, not clergy. This ministry should be trained for, recognized, and supported in ways the church has yet to learn to do.

Others will exercise that special calling as pastors of churches. They are ordained to that specific ministry. The New Testament indicates the pastor's functions and standing in the church:

1. Shepherd of the flock, hence the term "pastor" (Ephesians 4:11; see also Acts 20:28; 1 Peter 5:1-3);
2. Preacher and teacher (1 Timothy 5:17; Titus 1:9);
3. Healer (James 5:14-15);

4. Administrator (1 Timothy 5:17; Acts 15 gives examples of administrative decisions);

5. A position of respect (Hebrews 13:7, 17; 1 Peter 5:5; 1 Thessalonians 5:12-13; 1 Timothy 5:17);

6. A servant leader, following the example of Christ (Philippians 2:5-7; Luke 22:27);

7. Further, pastors were seen as God's *gifts* to the church. The New Testament clearly understood that the ministry of apostles, prophets, evangelists, *pastors,* and teachers was *given* for the purpose of equipping God's people for their own work of Christian service and "for building up the body of Christ" (Ephesians 4:11-12).

> The ministries mentioned by the apostle were Christ's gift to his church—part of his gift of the comforter which flowed from Pentecost. They were to be received not as an imposition and a burden (cf. 1 Corinthians 9), not as little divinities (cf. Acts 14:8ff.), but as gifts in the Holy Spirit from Christ, the Lord of the Church.[1]

It must also be seen that while pastors were held in high esteem as God's gifts, they were "first among equals." They were not separate from the people of God. They remained a part of the *laos.* They belonged to the body in which all members had important functions. Theirs was a *mutual* ministry, a ministry that was the ministry of the church. We can say, therefore, that today a pastor's credentials and authority to minister come from the church. His or her ministry is based in, undergirded by, and operates as an extension of the church. Pastors cannot operate as Lone Rangers. They need the support of, and to be accountable to, the church.

The Need for a Pastoral Relations Committee

Support for a minister takes place in many informal ways in the church: the simple thank-you note, the affirmation of a Sunday sermon, the trust invested in a minister in the context of a counseling session, invitations to dinner or social events. Yet, at the annual salary and benefits review and in times of hostile behavior toward the pastor, informal support is not enough. A specific, formal, recognized support system is necessary.

Also, there is an accountability on the part of the pastor. It is absolutely necessary for the pastor to be held accountable to the church in terms of ministerial role and function according to the contract. The best vehicle for providing formal support and maintaining the pastor's accountability is not the congregation, acting as a committee of the whole, nor even the church board or diaconate. It is the pastoral relations committee.

I served as executive minister of the Minnesota Baptist Conference for a decade. The most constantly occurring and difficult task was to moderate church fights, often between the pastor and the church. I think it is safe to say that if those churches, in which such rifts occurred, had had functioning pastoral relations committees, most of the problems could have been faced and handled before they had grown out of control like a cancer.

The "after-the-honeymoon" syndrome is all too real. During the pastor's first six months the people look excitedly at their church and new pastor. The sermons seem fresh and relevant. New programs are inaugurated. But then inherent flaws in both partners of this marriage begin to show up. People begin to realize that the pastor is not perfect. The pastor may be disappointed in people or programs.

When this happens, someone needs to talk *to* the pastor, not *about* the pastor. I had to spend an inordinate amount of time with one church after the pastor's first year. The pastor and church members were simply fighting over the congregation's perception of the pastor's willingness to call in their homes. "Our last pastor always did." There was no agreed-upon expectation. If a six-month review had been held by a pastoral relations committee, the pastor could have been informed of the congregation's concern. Early awareness of the issue could have resulted in an understanding between the pastor and the diaconate about their expectations for pastoral visitation of members.

A basic need for a pastor is to have an ombudsman in times of hostility. The pastorate is a lonely place, make no mistake about it. Strained relationships are inevitable. People take potshots at the pastor. "In a recent survey of over one hundred clergy, spouses, and members of religious orders . . . , 81 percent said they occasionally experienced hostile, blaming criticism. Twenty-five percent affirmed that this was the single most difficult personal problem they had to manage."[2] The pastoral relations committee can act as ombudsman for the pastor and provide a system for dealing with problems.

Again, who in your church has concern for the pastor's personal and family well-being? Who knows the special burdens he or she faces? Who actively promotes adequate salary and benefits for the minister? Who is concerned about a good, continuing education program that upgrades and revitalizes the pastor's ministry? These are some of the needs a functioning pastoral relations committee can address.

Dr. Robert D. Rasmussen, writing for the American Baptist Churches in the U.S.A. Commission on the Ministry, gives a good purpose statement for a pastoral relations committee: "The purpose of the Pastoral Relations Committee is to foster constructive communication between the congregation and its pastoral leadership and to implement the congregation's responsibility for its pastor's professional and personal well-being." [3] Through such a committee the people of the church have a forum for sharing their concerns regarding pastoral ministry, and the pastor has an arena in which issues can be dealt with fairly. The committee provides honest advocacy for the pastor.

Establishing and Organizing the Committee

Rasmussen also notes eight important areas involved in establishing and organizing a church pastoral relations committee. [4]

Official Standing

The committee needs to be "owned" by the congregation as part of its system of operation. Therefore, inclusion in the bylaws seems the best route to follow (especially, as I shall suggest later, if it becomes the core of the pastoral search committee). Short of that, congregational or board action should establish the committee.

Accountability

There are liabilities in assigning this function to an existing board, such as the diaconate.

First, the diaconate is usually too large for this purpose. Second, the diaconate's proper responsibility for the church's life and program would likely squeeze this concern into a small time slot on its agenda. Third, the pastor is not likely to be as candid with his or her governing board as with a smaller, nonthreatening committee. Fourth, the Committee ought to be more broadly representative of the congregation, not of just one board.[5]

The committee could be a subcommittee of the diaconate or of the church board, but the best arrangement seems to be that it be a separate standing committee. A separate committee would need, however, to report periodically to the diaconate or church board.

Care must be taken to maintain the unique, pastor relationship focus of the committee and not allow the committee to infringe upon the programmatic and administrative functions of the church board or diaconate by becoming a mini church board.

Membership Qualifications

Unquestionably, unique persons are called for. They should be respected, committed Christians who are discreet, caring, sensitive, supportive of the pastor, and at the same time confrontational, emotionally mature, patient, and flexible. Both men and women, young and old, ought to be on the committee.

My experience in working with churches in trouble has been that often the situations have evidenced the presence of a small group of dominating people who felt that they ran the church. Regardless of whether they were in positions of elected leadership, they held court in their homes after the business meeting and exerted great power. Obviously, persons of this kind are not truly supportive of the pastoral office and are not helpful to have on the committee.

Size of the Committee

Three to five persons ought to be on the committee. The genius of the committee's ability to function well is in its small size.

Selection Process, Term of Service, and Chairperson

It may be that the usual practice which uses the nominating committee, with the pastor as an *ex officio* member, will work in forming a pastoral relations committee. But one pastor has said that each year the diaconate chairperson simply appoints the committee in full consultation with the pastor.

Membership should be for a three-year term, with a third of the members going off in any given year. This same pastor, who has had experience with such committees for twenty-one years, goes on to indicate that this is the only committee in his church on which members can succeed themselves. The general rule would allow anyone to serve two three-year terms. The committee elects its own chairperson.

Frequency of Meeting

Definite dates should be set in advance for at least two meetings per quarter. (In the case of meeting for the first annual review, that date should be set in the letter or call to a new pastor.) "The very fact that a definite and regular time has been set will make it possible to deal with minor difficulties before they develop into major problems in the life of the church."[6] Roy M. Oswald tells of a pastor who saw his committee as a support group and met with the three members from 5:00-5:45 P.M. every Thursday "for the first six months of his transition. Meeting weekly, he was able to share what was going on with him on a regular basis, and receive feedback from them on a regular basis."[7]

Pastor's Relationship to the Committee

The pastor and other professional staff members should not be official members of the Committee, although they would be expected to participate in its sessions. The relationship is one of full mutuality and requires the pastor's input.

Only in extremely rare instances would a Committee be likely to declare an executive session from which the pastor is excused. Practically, the Committee cannot accomplish its purpose without the close cooperation of the pastoral leadership.[8]

Confidentiality

So *sensitive* is the nature of the committee's work that it goes without saying that discussion that transpires within the committee must be absolutely confidential. Minutes, if kept, should list only decisions, and these should not be widely shared.

The Work
of the Committee

2

The Agenda

Once the committee is established, the committee's work is enormous and therefore requires regularly scheduled meetings. The committee cannot simply wait for problems to arise before planning a meeting. Since the committee is small (three to five persons was suggested as optimum size in chapter 1), it should not be hard to plan at least eight meetings per year.

As we shall see in this chapter and in chapter 3, there are some special concerns that arise when a pastor arrives and when a pastor leaves. These concerns need careful handling by the committee.

A *yearly* agenda, however, needs to cover these areas:

1. "In-Service" training for the committee members on a continuing basis, including meeting with a consultant, reading materials in the field (see Appendix A), and discussing insights that are learned from reading.

2. Developing a system of support by developing a problem-solving process for handling complaints and by understanding stress.

3. Annual performance review.

4. Annual compensation review.

5. Provision for, and review of, continuing education plans.

6. Program for the enlistment of persons for the ministry.

The committee chairperson, in consultation with the pastor, needs to

17

develop a calendar of when these matters will come up on the agenda for the year's scheduled meetings. (Such a calendar is called a PERT chart.) Some items, such as the annual review and the performance review, will likely be handled at the end of the year and will take the entire meeting time. The initial discussion of the pastor's plan for continuing education will likewise take a whole meeting.

A regular meeting might have this agenda:

1. Prayer time.
2. "Getting on board" (members sharing what has been happening in their lives).
3. Agenda review.
4. In-service training time.
5. Reports on assignments (e.g., progress on the plan for highlighting the need for persons to be open to God's ministry).
6. A *regular* process for hearing praises and complaints and handling conflict.

Know the Field

There are few committees within the church that require the kinds of skills and knowledge of the field that the pastoral relations committee does. In addition to the personal traits described in the last chapter, it is also desired that committee members read widely and, if possible, attend workshops in the field. Appendix A gives a suggested bibliography. The committee needs to understand something about such areas as church administration, management by objectives, time management, the appropriate roles of the minister, special issues of termination emotions (emotions a pastor feels at the termination of a pastorate), clergy "burnout," up-to-date salary and benefits levels in the community, personnel review and evaluation systems, and conflict management. Of course, each committee person cannot be an expert in all areas, but each member can be assigned the task of knowing several areas well. This kind of investment works well with the recommended time of service for committee members—at least two three-year terms, with the opportunity for each member to succeed himself or herself. When the committee is set up, it might be well for a consultant or a representative from the denomination to meet with the group at its first meeting.

While the committee serves as a sounding board to the pastor, it also becomes a helpful interpreter of the pastor's role and the contract that has been agreed upon by the pastoral search committee and the board. Periodic written and oral reports of the negotiated roles should be made to the church.

Support Group for the Pastor

As already indicated, it is important for the pastor to have a collegial support group with which he or she can be open. Pastor Edward W. Pierce III, writing in the November, 1980, issue of *Minister*, says, "The need we feel for support grows out of the problems of distance that occur almost by the very nature of ministry itself." [1]

Providing Overall Collegiality

A support group made up of other pastors is not always possible; even though the pastor does have such a group, the pastoral relations committee functions in a unique way (and with some power to effect important changes) as a support to the pastor.

A good support system offers us two things—blankets and sandpaper. A good support community should offer us protection and affirmation at certain times in our life, as well as rubbing us the wrong way if that's what we need to be pushed onto our growing edge again. . . . A good support system contains three elements:
  1) Survival—helps us get out of trouble.
  2) Stability—gives us a sense of continuity of values, tradition, etc.
  3) Prodding—gets us moving when we've become lazy and complacent and need to begin struggling with issues again, both internally and externally. [2]

The committee has demonic possibilities also.

Many professional clergypersons have access to a pastoral/ministerial relations committee, but unfortunately it may not be designed as a support system. In fact many church leaders have endured a great deal of harassment and conflict in the context of such groups. So much so, in some instances, that these committees have been ignored or disbanded because of suspicion and fear." [3]

Process is important for a good support system. Pastor Pierce goes on to indicate:

The type of process with which I have had the best success is the problem-solving variety. In this arrangement, there is a problem poser who defines the issue as succinctly as possible, a facilitator who acts as a clarifier and maintains the process; and problemsolvers who compose the rest of the group, seeking to elaborate and support the issue by suggesting various alternatives and solutions.[4]

Aiding in a Transitional Period

The work of the committee begins the day the new pastor arrives. Getting off on the right foot in the new parish is important; in fact for the production of its book, *New Beginnings: Pastorate Start Up Workbook*, the Alban Institute built its work on the hypothesis that "the first 18 months of a new ministry will by and large determine the entire ministry of a Pastor in a given parish."[5]

The committee needs to understand and to interpret the power of termination emotions.[6] A pastor's own feelings about the place he or she has left are probably more powerful than is admitted or understood. Extra time with the family is necessary at the start up because of the *family members'* terminal emotions and because at least at the beginning they *are* the pastor's primary support group.

Not least in the area of termination emotions is the grief reaction of the new congregation (we shall deal more with this in the next chapter, "The Work of the Committee When a Pastor Leaves"). The congregation is dealing with denial, anger, and guilt, and as a result, through no fault of the new pastor, some members will leave. Both pastor and church need the valuable interpretation the committee can give at this point. (It would be wise for the committee to provide the pastor with the notebook, *New Beginnings,* from the Alban Institute, and encourage the pastor to work through it in the first months of his or her ministry.)

In addition to the grief of leaving a place, moving itself is a major crisis. It is no small wonder that pastors and their families undergo stress during the first eighteen months of the pastorate. A pastor's physical and psychological reactions need to be understood and he or she must be supported. A committee, alive to all of the emotions a new pastor experiences, can support a pastor and find that by working through these emotions with its pastor, it can establish a rapport and authenticity that will enhance its relations with the pastor for an entire pastorate.

The committee must be aware that the first months of a pastorate are needed simply to get started. The pastor and family have tasks such as moving in (the task of arranging the home is always enormous), becoming acquainted with the area, registering children for school, registering for a driver's license, voting. And the pastor needs to make entry into his or her new job which is quite unlike other professions. He or she is the pastor to a group of people, a relationship that requires an accountability, leadership, and intimacy as no other profession does. The history of the congregation's life must be learned. This involves far more than merely reading a written document. It includes such things as hearing and learning about what is valued, about the "heroes" of the faith, and the theological assumptions of persons in the congregation in general. A plan for ministry can be developed only *after* some months on the field. In the midst of all of these tasks, the pastor is often deluged with requests for speaking engagements from day one.

Fielding the Flak

Sooner or later flak comes. Pastors are especially vulnerable because their personal identity and faith are tied together. An attack on the pastor is an attack on his or her total existence. There are signals which say that the game of "Let's Get the Pastor" is on, writes G. Lloyd Rediger of the Wisconsin Council of Churches:

1. When one person, family, or small group of persons dominate the church's program and/or policymaking.
2. When a church has a history of short pastorates or frequent eviction of pastors.
3. When there are one or a few persons who pledge most of the church's income.
4. When there are strong conflicts within the church and the pastor is identified with one of the parties to the conflict.
5. When the church is in a downward trend in attendance, budget, or program.
6. When denominational executives in the area do not give strong support to pastors.
7. When the pastor tends to set himself [or herself] up for attack by unpopular crusades, truculent behavior, laziness or failing to perform legitimate pastoral duties, self denigration or constant violation of local church/ community customs.
8. When a church becomes ingrown. (This leads to "Groupthink"— when new or outside ideas are not allowed.)

9. When church members or pastor or denominational officials see church conflicts as win/lose struggles.[7]

Complaints against the pastor ought to be fielded immediately. Here is the test of the authenticity of the committee members and the committee process. *Communication* and *trust* are key components. If the pastor has confidence in the committee as his or her *ombudsman,* then he or she can hear the criticisms and know that together the conflict can be managed.

The value of frequent meetings of the committee and the pastor is apparent here. The committee must *hear* and handle criticisms firmly before the situation becomes impossible. For instance, when there is a downward trend in attendance or giving and the pastor becomes the scapegoat, the congregation needs to be reminded that the ministry of the church is a shared responsibility of all the people. When it is apparent that the Sunday sermons are poorly prepared and there is a laxity in the performance of pastoral duties, *trustworthy* persons can work with the pastor to establish personal growth and work patterns that can change this. And, of course, early diagnosis of a problem that might build to explosion can allow for a denominational executive or conflict consultant to be on the scene to help manage the crisis before it becomes unmanageable. Too often, churches let the problem stew until the only recourse is for the smallest group in the conflict to leave—namely, the pastor and family.

Conflict and How to Handle It

The use of a conflict consultant is usually reserved for the impossible situation and so the committee needs to develop its own expertise for managing conflict. Two good practical resources are Speed B. Leas, *A Lay Person's Guide to Conflict Management,* and chapter 5 of Richard Rusbuldt's *Basic Leader Skills.*[8]

The two basic areas of conflict in the church seem to be: "(a) the role of the pastor with its many different relationships; (b) the need for, or the results of, change."[9]

Conflict over the expectations of the pastoral role is clearly managed best by having a *contract* (written and agreed upon by the pastor and board in a group process, early in the pastor's ministry) which can be referred to when conflict arises. Change is unforeseen and probably is the item that generates the greatest conflict because change usually affects all or most of the church.

Warnings which tell us that conflict is brewing in the church are such indices as long, drawn-out, personally unfulfilling meetings; an increase of angry language; a win/lose attitude in decision making; a block of pledges not being paid; and changing friendship patterns.[10]

Richard Rusbuldt gives twelve practical suggestions on how to deal with differences:

1. When two persons (or groups) can discover and agree on what the real problem is, and view it as a common problem (both persons or groups owning it), you have made significant progress toward a solution.
2. Small fires, left unattended, become large fires if there is fuel to feed them. Deal with the sparks before they burst into full flames.
3. Deal with one issue at a time.
4. Be sure that full communication (two-way) is taking place with all persons or groups involved in the conflict.
5. Do not threaten or intimidate persons.
6. Deal with real issues, rather than dealing with personalities.
7. Facts are important. When each person or group involved in differences has all the facts, the possibilities increase greatly for full understanding to take place.
8. The feelings of the other person (or group) are equally as important as yours.
9. When tension or conflict heightens, feelings often become more important than facts.
10. Emphasize and use a caring, friendly attitude.
11. Search for "win-win" solutions, rather than "win-lose" responses.
12. Make decisions (no matter how small or great) by consensus rather than by vote, unless mandated to do so by your organization's charter.[11]

In the process of handling conflict, when one side wins and the other side loses, those who lose tend to back away and leave. If both sides lose, wounds are left from which the whole church suffers. In the "win-win" approach an attempt is made to discover solutions that can give satisfaction to both parties.

The *first step* in getting win-win results is to clarify and understand the differences which exist between persons or groups. *Identification* of the *real problem* is the first step to finding a meaningful solution.

Second, a commitment to finding a solution needs to be made by *both* sides. A high level of confidence, trust, loyalty, and candor needs to be created among the group's members as well as loyalty to the church as a whole. This is an important responsibility for the person who moderates or chairs the group.

Third, a commitment to meaningful communication must be made. Both sides must be kept in touch. Both sides need to have frequent dialogue. Doors to communication must be kept open. When a situation is critical, long periods of time between meetings may be counter-productive.

Fourth, consider all the possibilities for solutions available to both sides in the issue. Sometimes, in order for this to happen effectively, an outsider needs to be invited to provide clarity and objectivity to the situation. All the possible options for a solution should be investigated in order to determine which will be the most effective.

Fifth, each side in the issue should be committed to work as long as is necessary to discover the solution(s) to which both sides can agree.[12]

Coping with Burnout and the Sources of Stress

The dictionary defines *burnout* as "to fail, wear out, or become exhausted by making excessive demands on energy, strength, or resources." People in the helping professions have been talking about burnout for the past few years and recognize its symptoms to be insomnia, loss of appetite (or overeating), muscular tension, headaches, rashes, rapid heartbeat, frenzied activity (or lethargy), anger, indecisiveness, apathy, or irritability.[13]

Writes Rebecca E. Hight, "Prolonged and unrelieved stress may produce major illnesses or bring about the phenomenon known as the burnout syndrome."[14] Major source areas of stress are four:

1) attempting to meet the needs of many individuals,
2) tensions within a group,
3) the action of outside forces,
4) unrealistic self-expectations.[15]

A pastor faces all four. And the problem is that pastors are dedicated to caring for people and often cannot say no to a request for help. They run the risk of the "messiah complex"; attempting to meet the needs of others and having unrealistic expectations of themselves can kill them.

Some Stress Factors Unique to Clergy

Everyone faces stress, but there are some situations of stress that

Roy Oswald feels are unique to clergy. He has adapted the stress survey conducted by Dr. Thomas H. Hulmes of The University of Washington and has listed fifty-seven clergy stress factors, giving them each a relative value on a one-hundred-point scale. See the chart that follows.

As the committee reviews the stress factors periodically (perhaps at least at the annual review), let the members ask themselves what factors may now be influencing their pastor. Without the committee's prying, and in the climate of the trust relationship so absolutely necessary between the pastor and committee, stress factors should be recognized and understanding, support, and counsel given.

CLERGY STRESS FACTORS

Event	Scale Value
Death of spouse	100
Divorce	73
Marital separation	65
Death of close family member	63
Personal injury or illness	53
Marriage	50
Serious decline in church attendance	49
Segment of congregation meeting privately to discuss your resignation	47
Marital reconciliation	45
Retirement	45
Change in health of family member	44
Pregnancy	40
Sex difficulties	39
Alienation from one's Board/Council/Session/Vestry	39
Gain of new family member	39
Change in financial state	38
Death of close friend	37
Increased arguing with spouse	35
Merger of two or more congregations	35
Children in stress	33
Parish in serious financial difficulty	32
Mortgage over $10,000	31
Difficulty with member of church staff (Associates, Organist, Choir Director, Secretary, Janitor, etc.)	31
Foreclosure of mortgage or loan	30
Church burns down	30
Son or daughter leaving home	29
Trouble with in-laws	29

An influential church member irate over something you did	29
Slow, steady decline in church attendance	29
Outstanding personal achievement	28
Introduction of new hymnal to worship service	28
Failure of church to make payroll	27
Remodeling or building program	27
Wife begins or stops work	26
Begin or end school	26
Death of peer	26
Receiving a call to another parish	26
Change in living conditions	25
Revision of personal habits	24
Former pastor active in parish in negative way	24
Difficulty with Confirmation Class	22
Change in residence	20
Change in schools	20
Change in recreation	19
Change in social activities	18
Death/Moving away of good church leader	18
Mortgage or loan less than $10,000	17
Change in sleeping habits	16
Change in family reunions/get togethers	15
Change in eating habits	15
Stressful continuing education experience	15
Major program change	15
Vacation	13
Christmas	12
Lent	12
Easter	12
Minor violations of the law	11 [16]

The committee needs to watch for signs of burnout and counsel the pastor, helping him or her to face honestly the fact that he or she cannot save the whole world. Practical matters such as calendaring "time-out" activities, exercise time, and sufficient time for themselves will help pastors to reduce stress.

Of course the problem of stress may go deeper. The pastor may be a workaholic. This is defined by Wayne Oates as one who has an "addiction to work, the compulsion or the uncontrollable need to work incessantly." [17] That may require some in-depth counseling, but the habit can be kicked! The committee would do well to read Oates's delightful book *Confessions of a Workaholic*.

The Pastor's Spouse and Stress

Lost in the shuffle sometimes is the pastor's spouse. Beverly Ann Croskery, reporting on "The Wife's View of Parish Life," from a survey done by the Academy of Parish Clergy shows some deep problem areas, which, when ranked, include:

1. congregation's demands on husband's time
2. financial insecurity
3. lack of social life outside the church
4. pressures on children
5. living in a manse
6. life in a goldfish bowl
7. and 8. tied: double standard expected, and trapped feeling
9. poor self image
10. frustration in conforming to expected life style
11. expectation to give service without financial reward
12. jealousy of time and talent on the part of parishioners
13. need to accept special favors and discounts
14. unfair treatment by parishioners[18]

Increasing numbers of clergy divorces may indicate the severity of these fourteen frustrations. The pastoral relations committee needs to be sensitive to these pressures that the pastor's spouse and family face.

Performance Review

Theologian Hans Kung has shown in his treatment of the priestly office that all ministry is reponsible to the church as a whole. In the Protestant church the pastor is invested with the authority to act on behalf of the church. With that authority, there is also an accountability.

Clearly, the pastoral relations committee needs to address the matter of clergy accountability. While the matter is not the sole province of the committee (since performance review is the church board's or diaconate's responsibility), the pastoral relations committee, as the *continuing presence* of the committee that called and covenanted with the pastor in the first place, has the best grasp of the unwritten expectations of the congregation and the unwritten expectations of the new pastor at the time of the initial negotiations.

The function of the pastoral relations committee at this point is to *interpret* to the board and congregation what the pastor's expectations are or, at least, to sit with the pastor when his or her performance is being reviewed, formally or informally, to help clarify *accountability*. The pastor is accountable, but to what *standard* or agreements?

As a step toward clarification, Lyle Schaller suggests that the board at its first meeting after the new pastor's arrival set an agenda for arriving at an understanding of the pastor's "contract," which will later form the basis for review. Rarely can the written document of call contain the full understanding of all the mutual expectations of the ministerial role. This is finally worked out as an understanding, based on answers to the following questions.

1. How much "routine" calling in the homes of members do the people believe is expected of the pastor?
2. How much time does the contract call for the minister to spend on denominational and interdenominational responsibilities?
3. Does your . . . contract call for the pastor to be one of the leaders in the congregation? Or to be *the* leader?
4. What is understood to be the responsibility of the pastor for the planning, organization and implementation of the Christian education program of the church?
5. What is understood to be the pastor's responsibility for the financial administration of the congregation?
6. Does the contract between your congregation and your pastor call for him [her] to be *the* evangelist for the congregation?
7. How high is the priority given to sermon preparation?
8. How high is the priority given to the role of the pastor as a community leader?
9. If your congregation has an assistant or associate minister, to whom does he [she] turn for a periodic review of his/her "contract"?
10. Who reviews the total "compensation" package? To whom are their recommendations directed?
11. What is the most urgent item in the contract between your pastor and your congregation that deserves review as soon as possible?[19]

That first meeting of the board is very important as an immediate clarification of the expectations of the new pastor. This is why it is important that the pastoral relations committee be a part of the pastoral search committee in any church constitution. Often this is not the case, and the pastor who dealt with a pastoral search committee with no continuing life of its own is now faced with dealing with a group of people with whom he or she has not had the in-depth conversations and implicit agreements on expectations for ministry. This is a situation destined for great misunderstandings.

An important function of the committee, therefore, is to work with the board to interpret and clarify and then be part of each annual review. (See Appendix B for a suggested annual review.) As a support system, the committee works in an ongoing fashion to help the pastor reflect constructively on his or her work, evaluate strengths, discover weaknesses, and plan a systematic program to upgrade competencies.

Compensation Review

Galatians 6:6 is a good passage for churches to remember as they deal with a pastor's compensation: "Let him who is taught the word share all good things with him who teaches."

As part of the pastoral search committee, the pastoral relations committee had a part in negotiating the pastor's income, business expense, and fringe benefits. These are never set in concrete and must be reviewed annually in terms of the effects of inflation, merit, and length of service.

The Committee's function here seems three-fold:
a) Understanding what is adequate ministerial compensation,
b) Reviewing annually their pastoral leadership's compensation and making recommendations to the proper board(s) or finance committee, and
c) Education of congregational attitudes regarding ministerial compensation.[20]

Income

Salary. The pastor is a professional person. The day of the clergy discount for "poor pastors" is over. The salary can be arrived at through the use of two medians. The "community median" is found through examining the school board's salary scales and the chamber of commerce median income information for the community.[21] Many churches have found it useful to seek information about the salary levels of those who bring to their professions a comparable educational background. The "congregational median" can be found simply by asking the church board members to list their annual gross salaries, unsigned. In figuring the salary, one should also remember that pastors pay their own Social Security as self-employed persons.

A church should remember that a pastor incurs certain legitimate expenses in fulfilling his [her] service responsibility to God and the church. These

expenses should not be considered part of [the] salary but should be
accurately reflected in the format of the budget."[22]

Housing and utility allowance. If a parsonage and utility expenses
are provided, it is important that the house be kept in good repair and
that the church report the actual rental value to a retirement plan for
the purpose of determining pension premiums. If a housing allowance
is provided, it must be adequate for meeting the cost of family housing
in the community. The housing allowance is considered *excludable*
income under present IRS ruling when the pastor reports income for
tax purposes.

There are pros and cons on the subject of whether the church should
pay housing allowance or provide a parsonage for the pastor. Writes
Lyle Schaller,

> The church-owned parsonage or manse is an arrangement that exists *pri-
> marily* as a convenience to the *congregation,* not to the pastor. This is
> why the minister does not have to pay federal income tax on the value of
> his housing. Traditionally, the arrangement has been the result of the
> congregation's desire to have a resident minister.[23]

More and more, in urban areas especially, pastors are choosing a
housing allowance and are owning their own homes because of a number
of benefits they feel strongly about:

1. *Independence.* This is true even when the pastor uses the housing
allowance to rent a house. "This is our home." The pastor and spouse
have chosen it to meet *their* needs and tastes.

2. *Security.* The pastor and spouse feel they are making an investment
in their financial future by building equity in a house.

3. *Stability.* Pastors tend to sink their roots into their community
when they own a home there. They can be seen as and function as tax-
paying homeowners in that community.

There are cons about the matter of home ownership, some of which
few pastors see:

1. Mobility is reduced. It is more difficult to move, simply because
of the logistics of selling the house, and in a down market the Lord
may hardly lead the pastor to another place!

2. It is possible to lose a substantial amount on the house in a
declining market or if a person stays only a few years and builds little
or no equity.

3. Since most pastors have not been able to save very much and have few investments, the problem of a substantial down payment on a house is very real. Some churches make possible a low-interest loan reserve, kept always for that purpose. The loan need not be repaid until the pastor leaves and the house is sold.[24]

4. While there is the unspoken suggestion of freedom in the offer of a housing allowance, the pastor is not always as free as it may seem to live where he or she wants. Often the pastor will be expected to live where the majority of the congregation lives.

5. Often the housing allowance paid by the church is less than the cost of owning a home since when setting a housing allowance, hidden costs, such as utilities, phone, insurance, taxes, and especially repairs, may not adequately be taken into account.

If a house is not provided, *adequate* allowance should be paid. If the church provides a house, "the worth of the house or its cost should not be deducted from the pastor's income, since he [she] does not own it and will have no equity in it . . ."[25] when leaving. The principal value of the house, what would be received by sale, is the true value to the pastor.

Business Expenses

Auto expenses. This is clearly an operating cost of the church and in *no way* should be considered part of the salary. Some churches lease a car and ask the pastor to pay for personal travel in it. Others pay mileage at a level equal to the IRS mileage allowance. And many churches pay a flat amount.

Denominational conferences and meetings. Sending the pastor to these events is part of the church's investment in the denominational life and is clearly a part of ministerial work. Travel costs, room, per diem food allowances and registration fees should be budgeted. Some churches prefer to pay actual costs. When a conference is some distance away, the cost of air travel should be allowed regardless of the mode of travel the pastor elects to use.

Continuing education expenses. Continuing education will be discussed as a special function of the pastoral relations committee but the necessity for adequately budgeting this as an operating expense item yearly is important. *The value to the church is incalculable.*

Hospitality allowance. Most pastors spend out-of-pocket money entertaining prospective members, guest speakers, and others. To make some provision, however small, in the budget, says that the church takes note of this expense and is grateful for the ministry.

Fringe Benefits

Group health insurance. This is a must for the minister and family. Most denominations have such a plan. It is important to review the policy carefully and ask if it provides for such benefits as life insurance, accidental death and dismemberment, long-term disability income, educational benefits for children (at the death of the minister), hospitalization costs, surgical, maternity, in-hospital doctor's calls, and major medical. Premium costs are paid directly by the church.

Retirement plan. Again, most denominations today have a suggested retirement plan. If a pastor chooses to elect his or her own plan, the church should always pay the premiums directly. If this is not possible, the church should demand that the retirement premiums budgeted for are definitely spent on a retirement plan.

Church members may cringe at the amounts of salary, business expenses, and fringe benefits. However, they are real costs, and the church must see them as the price of adequate ministerial work and part of the church's mission.

Smaller churches, of course, have less with which to work, but efforts toward providing these costs must continually be made. A full explanation to the prospective pastor and full disclosure of church finances will help him or her to understand the situation in a clearer way and to determine his or her acceptance of the call. It should be the pastoral relations committee's task yearly to evaluate the situation and press for adequate remuneration.

Continuing Education

In a rapidly changing world the ministry, along with all professions, needs continuing education. And, more than persons of any other profession, the minister cannot afford to become stale.

Industry has learned that the key to creativity and greater job satisfaction is not working conditions, status, or salary. These are the environmental factors, which, if missing, are keys to job *dissatisfaction.*

What motivates job *satisfaction* and creativity is the *challenge of the task*.[26]

Too often pastors, feeling stale in their work, will look for another call. This may not be the answer. Increasing the salary may cause him or her to stay but will not necessarily motivate the pastor to creativity and job satisfaction. One key is a regular performance review, which can provide the kind of feedback that motivates. And just as important, writes Richard J. Kirk, "is to allow and encourage involvement, on a regular basis, in programs of continuing education or better, of on-the-job consultation. These can broaden horizons, stimulate thinking, and enable the pastors to expand and increase professional skills."[27]

Workshops, a study travel leave, Monday classes at a seminary, and an intentional five-year plan for professional enrichment were redeeming for me in a twelve-year pastorate in Minneapolis. Reading Mark Rouch's book *Competent Ministry: A Guide to Effective Continuing Education* was a revolutionary experience. He delineated three kinds of learning: *Lifelong, basic formal,* and *continuing. Lifelong learning* is an attitude, a dimension of living that "lets learning occur anytime, anywhere."[28] *Basic formal education* is the education qualifying one for ordination. Obviously, by definition, this has already been accomplished for good or bad and cannot be repeated. *Continuing education is an individual's personally designed learning program which begins when basic formal education ends and continues throughout a career and beyond. An unfolding process, it links together personal study and reflection and participation in organized group events.*[29]

Rouch lists five educational "events," which, purposefully linked together, form continuing education:

1. *Individual study and reflection.* The trick is to learn to do this in the midst of the pressures of family, job, and the knowledge explosion.

2. *Local groups.* A variety of group learning events that require no break in one's regular routine and that can range from congregational consultation-training events to study groups with professional colleagues or with laity.

3. *Short-term organized courses and seminars.* These last from three to ten days and are usually close to home.

4. *Long-term programs.* These last three to nine months and, like sabbaticals, require a leave of absence and usually a change of residence. The newest trend in seminary education is "distance learning," where a person can take seminary courses (even toward a D.Min. degree) via modern technology.

5. *Planning*. Put together, the first four events provide a program of education, but randomly participating in various episodes is not continuing education. The key to continuing education is planning it.[30]

It is a function of the pastoral relations committee to encourage the pastor to do a five-year plan for personal and professional enrichment, to seek help (funding and adequate time) from the church for it, and to require periodic accountability and possible adjustments in the program. The plan needs to ask four questions in logical sequence.

1. *What do I need personally and professionally?*
2. *What resources are available?*
3. *What are the reality factors?* Factors such as time, money, family, recent or impending job change, and availability of certain programs all modify the ideal.
4. *What is being accomplished?* If the definition of education is to produce change, we need to ask periodically if we have changed as we learn.[31]

More and more congregations are understanding continuing education to be a practical part of the working year and not a vacation. Many congregations are offering a three- to six-month sabbatical study leave with pay (and a stipend for study costs) after five to seven years of service. Apart from the learning component of such a sabbatical, "however a minister spends his/her sabbatical, it is clearly a respite from the taxing routine of preaching, counseling, administration and the other functions that, after several years, constitute a sort of treadmill."[32] It is in fact a respite in depth, different from an annual vacation. It provides the pastor a time away for reflection and study. I can attest to such an event's literally redeeming consequences!

Enlistment of Persons for the Ministry

Someone has said that "the church is always within one generation of extinction." It needs to keep telling the story, winning new people to faith in Jesus Christ and to a life of discipleship through the church. A nonrecruiting church has no future. The same must be said about pastoral leadership. "Any congregation that utilizes professional leaders is obligated to assist in their discovery, encouragement, and education."[33] The pastoral relations committee is the group within the church that, by nature of its very task, has a stake in the recruitment of future ministers. Concern for keeping the sense of "call to the ministry" alive in the congregation is a valid function of the committee. With the pastor, it can seek to identify those persons whose gifts lie in the direction of professional church leadership, counseling them to be aware of God's call and what preparation for ministry entails.

It is part of the historic free church tradition that the congregation be aware of, encourage, and support those whose gifts and calling are towards the ministry. Giving opportunities to exercise those gifts of speaking and service is part of the process. Some churches have set aside scholarship funds to help support their own members in the long seven-year preparation for professional church leadership. If it had not been for the concern, confirmation of a call, counsel, and deep support of the members of the little Baptist church in Chisholm, Minnesota, I would not be in the ministry today. Theirs was an abiding concern that they would thrust forth sons and daughters for the "full-time" service of Christ. While there was no pastoral relations committee, the needs for future church leadership was strongly emphasized by the diaconate through the whole life of the church. They were intentional about it. This intentionality is easily lost and belongs rightly as a valid concern of the pastoral relations committee.

The Work of the Committee When a Pastor Leaves

Some years ago it was estimated that between one-fourth and one-third of all congregations in American Protestantism would bid farewell to their minister.[1] Most farewells will mark the moving of the pastor to another church. Some will be "rites of passage" to retirement, and in approximately four hundred churches the farewells will be at the pastor's funeral.

Since most pastors resign to take another church, it is assumed that they have arrived at an understanding that their work is done. However, that mystic "will of God" is difficult to comprehend at any juncture in life, not the least of which being the point of determining that one's ministry is now complete in this particular church.

Gerald Gillaspie, in his excellent book *The Restless Pastor,*[2] points out that negative indications for leaving may be *disappointment*—the strong feeling that pastor and people are no longer suited for each other; *discouragement*—there seems to be no progress and conditions seemingly cannot be overcome; *opposition*—a hostile element constitutes more than 10 percent of the membership (especially if it includes leaders); *insufficient salary* for the growing needs of the family; *dissatisfaction*—measured by such indices as falling attendance and decreasing financial contributions; and *a demand for resignation* by the church.

Positive indications of pastoral change may be *success*—the pastor has done well and is ready for another opportunity; *challenge*—the pastor wants a larger opportunity (not necessarily a larger church or salary); *attitude*—special gifts the pastor is now aware of and has honed to a great degree of effectiveness may cause him or her to think of a ministry that best uses these skills; *health and family needs*—a doctor or professional person suggests a change.

Sometimes a pastor resigns for no other reason than a sense of "call" to another field. The pastor is not restless and does not need to go, but a persistent pulpit committee challenges him or her to come to its church.

At no time is the role of the pastoral relations committee so critical as when a pastor leaves, for whatever reason. This is a tremendous time of transition. Let us review some of the critical points of the process.

Resignation to Take Another Church

A committee can help the pastor at the junction of *entertaining a call*. Seldom should a pastor resign without another call or job offer. The call-less pastor is suspect and often has great difficulty getting a call.

When the Pastor Entertains a Call

When the pastor receives a call, there is usually a fair span of time from the first overtures of a church to the pastor to his or her formal resignation and acceptance of the call.

It is best that the pastor take the pastoral relations committee into his or her confidence as soon as he or she becomes serious about a possible call. (Ethics are demanded here; no one should use the possibility of a call or letter of call to better one's present position. This can be a deadly kind of pressure.) No pastor should candidate without letting a church leader know. Unusual circumstances may dictate otherwise, but early notification should be the norm. The pastor should not sneak off. Few things make a church angrier than to find out that the pastor went to candidate without telling anyone. Further, ethics indicate that unless he or she is willing to take the day as a vacation Sunday, the pastor ought to offer to pay for the pulpit supply in his or her absence.

The Formal Resignation

The church can learn formally that the pastor is leaving in a number of ways. The most sensible manner, it seems to me, is for the pastor to share the resignation with the church board or diaconate chairperson and the head of the pastoral relations committee and then to notify the whole church by mail. This is easier on pastor and people than informing the people in person and has the advantage that everyone learns about it at the same time.

A technical point to remember in the whole process of resignation is that the church need not act on the resignation. The resignation cannot be voted down; the pastor will go regardless. The vote is moot. If, under God and through prayer, the pastor has sensed God's call to leave, he or she will not reconsider. The church should understand that. The only action needed by the church is to note in the church minutes at the next business meeting that the pastor has resigned. The next action would be to form a pulpit committee.

The Grief of Resignation

Perhaps there is no relationship outside that of the immediate family in which one becomes so involved at a personal level as the relationship of a pastor and his or her congregation. The pastor has led many to faith in Jesus Christ, counseled people in difficult times, visited them when they were sick, married them, dedicated their children, and buried their loved ones. There is a trauma in the church when the shepherd says, "I am leaving." Church members, especially young persons who moved from childhood to adulthood while this pastor was there, personal friends, ministerial colleagues—all suffer loss.

Homer Carter, in his incisive article "The Grief in Leaving a Pastorate," speaks of accepting "the reality of death in this pastoral relationship."[3] In her book *The Minister Is Leaving* Celia A. Hahn entitles the section that deals with this area, "The Funeral."[4] Grief, therefore, is seen to be a natural and normal part of the process of resigning for both the pastor and people. For the minister's spouse and children, it may be even more difficult. I have known pastors' children for whom the move occurred the summer following graduation. They said that they had forever lost "home," as they had known it, and came to live in a new place with parents during school holidays, military furloughs, or vacations from work.

Carter describes the grief of the congregation through Jim Ewing's "phenomena" as outlined in his "Bereavement or Grieving process." There is *shock* and *panic,* a sometimes uncontrollable anxiety on the part of the congregation. "The church will go under. You can't leave now." *Denial* may appear. The thought of God's call is swept away; the church will offer a higher salary if only the pastor stays on. *Depression* may be part of the congregation's grief work. So closely is the pastor identified with the church's progress that it has no future without him or her. *Hostility* may rear its head. Few pastors are prepared for that grief reaction. Sometimes a church, having received the resignation, will move with alacrity to have the pastor off the field sooner than he or she wanted to leave. *Recovery* can be experienced and the farewell service can be a joyful rite of passage as the congregation understands the sovereign hand of God in it all.[5]

> It is highly unlikely that this grief of leaving will be dealt with adequately unless (a) . . . the existence of this grief is recognized and accepted as normal and (b) the list of those who feel the sense of grief is recognized as a long list of many different names. In a few cases the regional judicatory of the denomination is beginning to recognize and respond [creatively] to the fact that the [minister's] departure is a serious grief-producing experience for many people.[6]

Other Reactions to Resignation

Celia A. Hahn has isolated other reactions in her reflections on fourteen case histories.

1. *Anxiety, fear, panic*—These come from the thought that the ship may have no helmsman. The Diocese of Central New York's Handbook for Parishes in search of a rector points out that panic may be a normal reaction: "Expect panic on all sides from nearly everyone that the congregation will dry up and blow away unless a new rector is found tomorrow." There seems to be greater panic when there is a strong dependence upon the pastor, less when there is a strong lay leadership.

2. *Guilt and self-doubt*—Guilt can be felt over criticism one may have made against the pastor that may be causing the pastor to move. Persons can experience self-doubt in the same way that a child may feel partly to blame for the death of a parent.

3. *Anger*—This may occur especially if the pastor was forced out. Anger often is turned on persons who are perceived as the "ones who made pastor leave" and, hence, can leave deep scars.

4. *Understanding and self-confidence*—In a church with strong lay leadership, it appears that mature people, though sorry to lose a minister, may see it as the pastor's "graduation" to a new and perhaps greater opportunity.

5. *Sometimes feelings of relief* or even a lack of strong reactions seem natural in churches in which the pastorate had not been firmly established because of its temporary character, because of illness or frequent absence on the part of the minister, or because the clergyman's predecessor had not been "laid to rest." [7]

All of these are natural reactions. What is important "is for a congregation to be aware of, express, and deal with its own peculiar constellation of grief reactions before it is ready to embrace a new pastoral leadership." [8] Roy Oswald says that one of the most effective ways for the church to deal with its grief feelings is for the pastor to *model closure* for the people. If he or she handles closure well, the manner of dealing with endings can be "caught" by the congregation. [9] Resigning means the death of a minister's special role with that congregation. We will deal with this matter in the next chapter. But suffice it to say that a pastor's failure to die to the role of pastor to this church is what brings him or her back, after leaving, to continue to do pastoral acts. "To model termination is to be able to let go—and to be open and candid about the feelings that emerge in that letting go." [10]

Whether it be through the counsel and insight of a visit from a denominational judicatory person or through the pastoral relations committee, biblical understandings of the church and ministry must be lifted up to help the church members handle reactions to the pastor's leaving. One such understanding is that Christ is head of the church. The church is God's people and God wants the mission of the church maintained. God has not deserted.

Another is that all the people of God are ministers, and the church can perform its mission in the interim between pastors. A third biblical understanding is that no pastor is indispensible. Various gifts are needed. One plants, another waters in God's system. God will lead another pastor to this church.

Again, in cases of great grief or reaction to the loss of a pastor, a church needs the services of a seasoned interim pastor who is sensitive to that loss and can nurture a congregation through it.

"The Period in Between"

Between the time the pastor resigns and actually leaves the field, there is counsel and work of a unique nature for the pastoral relations committee. The period between giving the official resignation and actually leaving the field has sometimes been referred to as a "lame duck" time. Imperceptibly something changes. People realize that the minister is on his or her way, and the pastor may suddenly realize that his or her counsel on church policy is no longer sought; the church no longer revolves around him or her. This can be difficult if the pastor is not prepared for it, and it is one good reason to keep this period brief. Church constitutions sometimes demand a certain number of days' notice—usually thirty to sixty days. The pastor who resigns long in advance of his or her going usually wishes minimum notice had been given.

The Exit Interview

Many organizations find that an exit interview with employees who are leaving is very helpful. Schaller says that this kind of interview for a pastor is frequently conducted by an outside third party "in order to depersonalize the interpretation of what is said and to emphasize the constructive aspects of the departing minister's comments."[11] But if the pastoral relations committee has established a real rapport with the pastor, the interview can be done by the committee. The interview provides a time to speak candidly of issues, blockages to progress, and hopes and dreams. It may also be helpful for the pastor to define his or her role.

"Often the role of a minister changes between the first and last years in the same pastorate. It is *essential* for the lay leaders to have an up-to-date understanding of the role of the departing minister if they are to talk intelligently about the role of the next minister. Or, to be more precise, it is necessary to define the role of the departing minister in order to *redefine* the role expectations as these leaders talk expectations with potential candidates and/or the next minister."[12]

What the Pastor Should Leave

Nothing irks church leaders nor causes a rift between predecessors and successors in the ministry more than for the departing pastor to leave poor records, loose ends in terms of church affairs, or an untidy parsonage. Ministerial ethics and etiquette demand that things be in such an order that the new minister can begin to do the work of the ministry immediately instead of having to spend the first months sorting things out. A departing minister must live by the Golden Rule: things should be left as he or she would like to find them in the next church. (For a list of what to leave, see Appendix C.) A mutual understanding of such a standard by the pastor and committee is important.

Some Good Uses of Time

This period may not be only a "lame duck" time. The pastor should be helped to understand that it should not be wasted time. Granted, the pastor and spouse are already looking forward to the new field, to decorating a new home, and to packing. The present church, however, is paying the pastor's salary, and honest labor is still demanded. Positive sermons on the church and the economy of God, where "one sows and another waters," can be preached. Preparation of the church for the coming of the new pastor is needed, urging loyalty to him or her. Calling on people for the last time, praying for them, and urging those who have not made a commitment to Jesus Christ or joined the church to do so are some things the departing pastor can pursue.

It is *not* the function of the departing minister to work with the pastoral search committee. One does *not* help name one's successor. Nor is it the time to start new programs for one's successor to carry out!

Since the pastor's resignation has a ripple effect in a multiple-staff situation, it is necessary for the pastor to work through closure with the staff, but to understand that the board will *set* the tasks for the staff. The board may ask the pastor about staff assignments, but it is not the pastor's function to assign tasks. The reins are given at this point to the official church leadership.

A pastor must realize in this in-between period that he or she is leaving the roles, functions, and responsibilities and, in fact, is leaving the church. Promises of "I'll be back" should not be made. At this point, the pastor needs to read a denominational code of ethics. Someone has said, ''When you consider resigning a church, be sure you will; be sure you do; and be sure you did!''

John Fletcher, of the Alban Institute, says that terminally ill people have four major tasks to perform when they discover they will die soon:

1. They need to take control of what remains of their life . . . as opposed to passively letting others dictate the way they will die.
2. They need to get their affairs in order. . . .
3. They need to let old grudges go. . . .
4. They need to say ''thank you,'' to the people for whom they feel gratitude.[13]

Roy Oswald feels that this is precisely the closure task of the minister leaving the church. (*Running Through the Thistles: Terminating a Ministerial Relationship with the Parish* is a *must* reading for the pastoral relations committee.)

The Farewell Service

A farewell service is necessary from many points of view. It is, in fact, a rite of passage: a chapter is concluded; a new one is about to begin. The conclusion of ministry in this church must be made publicly and formally noted. The Christian community needs the opportunity to take note, to assess accomplishments, and to express gratitude. The farewell service may well be the final factor in the process of grief healing. Homer Carter writes in a deeply autobiographical way:

> The farewell service was extremely meaningful to me and to my wife. It ritualized the termination. It also lifted our leaving into a forward-movement process that freed us to celebrate the ongoingness of life for both pastor and people. The service was a ritual of integration. For the first time, the pastor and the congregation were together in their grief work.[14]

Some Suggestions

Avoid the maudlin, teary service. Tears will be there anyway. Do *not* sing '''Til We Meet At Jesus' Feet'' for the closing song!

The best time for the service seems to be Sunday afternoon or evening with a reception following, so that members of neighboring churches can be present.

The service should be one hour in length with no sermon. The pastor's farewell message can be delivered in the morning service.

Good music and the pastor's favorite songs are integral to the service.

The chairperson of the church should preside, with the church board chairperson, staff representative, and ministerial association representative giving remarks only.

Flowers for the pastor's whole family are appropriate. A love offering and/or gifts to the family members are especially meaningful.

Some churches have done a well-organized "This Is Your Life" program for the pastor or have shown slides of his or her ministry through those years being celebrated.

A Communion service might well be one of the best ways to show the deep *koinonia* which had been achieved in this pastorate.

The important thought that needs to order the mood of the service is that the pastor has been called by God to another place and this is not a tragedy. The service is a service of graduating or commissioning. Homer Carter, writing from a liturgical background, speaks of a farewell service for himself, planned by his wife: "The worship service moved forward around several focal points: an act of reverence, an act of gratitude, an act of commitment, an act of renewal, and an act of dedication." [15]

Leaving Under Duress

No marriage runs smoothly. Confrontations come, but no one can assume that confrontations are grounds for separation. Give the marriage of pastor and people a chance. The words "for better or for worse" from marriage vows have meaning here in the relationship of pastor and people. In marriages that last, the partners learn to accept the failings and flaws of each other. When the failures show up—as they surely will—mature people do not give up and do not ask for a divorce. To be sure, on rare occasions the realization that a mismatch has occurred is seen and the pastor leaves. The relationship of pastor and people is unique upon the face of the earth. To make it go, both parties have to work at it and both have to accept what the other brings to the union.

Sometimes, through arbitration by the committee and/or denominational staff, areas of disagreement or weakness can be isolated and contracts made. I have actually written out contracts whereby church leaders have agreed to do certain things and the pastor has agreed to keep his or her end of the bargain. Such a contract is written so that progress in areas of weakness can be measured: "The church board will take no further action towards dismissal but will stand behind the pastor publicly and privately"; "The pastor and spouse agreed to go through North Central Career Development Center for counsel"; or "He/she agrees to make ten calls per week and make monthly reports to the board." Three to six months later, I would appear at the church board meeting for an accounting from the board and pastor.

Sometimes negotiations do not work. The church is bigger than any of us and sometimes it becomes apparent that a pastor must leave or the church will be hopelessly polarized. It is the mark of integrity, out of the pastor's high regard of the church, for the pastor to encourage loyal followers who say, 'We'll leave if you do," to stay with the fellowship. In the church, scars can heal and old friendships mend. The Holy Spirit can bring true *koinonia* once again. In God's system where one sows and another waters, a new pastor can win the loyalty of all factions and bring healing to the body. One has to believe in the church and trust the Lord of the church to continue to build it.

The forced resignation is the hardest thing a pastor may face. It is easy for the pastor and his or her family to become very bitter. Careful interpretation of the situation to teenagers will keep them from throwing out their relationship to the church and even to Christ because "Dad or Mom was unfairly put out." How many preachers' kids today are no longer connected to the church because this happened to a parent? To vent one's spleen at the church in front of the family may carry a terribly high price tag later on.

This is also why it is necessary for church leaders to deal with this situation gently. They are dealing not only with the pastor but also with the children and spouse who only see their loved one being terribly hurt. If it becomes the talk of the town and of the school, young people are hurt even more.

Except in extreme cases, the pastor should not immediately resign with no place to go. Economics dictate that the family needs to eat. I have had good success with the concept of "intention to resign." The pastor notifies the church board of his or her intention to resign. It indicates that he or she is actively pursuing other calls and/or ministries.

Most people are gracious and will allow the time necessary for the process of finding work to take its course.

During this time it is *absolutely necessary* that the pastor and the pressure group agree to back off and not talk about the issues. The points are moot anyway. The pastor—right or wrong—will leave. There is no reason to continue to *prove* rightness or wrongness, capability or inability.

If a church cannot handle such an arrangement because it feels the pastor cannot stay in the pulpit one Sunday longer or if the pastor feels that emotionally he/she cannot continue to minister, termination should take place immediately. At this point the touchstone of how Christian the church is will be its treatment of the pastor financially. If he or she is forced to resign, a *minimum* of six months' salary and benefits should be offered, and if a parsonage is provided, the family ought to be allowed to occupy it for the same length of time, if needed. Few pastors will want to stay that long; so the church leaders need not fear. The group health plan must remain in effect as long as the pastor is on the payroll. This is important, especially if there is a health problem that might be excluded under a non-group plan.

Never does a pastor stand taller than when he/she is gracious under these trying circumstances. As the Master who, when reviled, did not revile, the pastor should not lash out at critics. He or she should preach the Word and not use the pulpit as a way of getting back at the pressure group. In fact, the pastor can ask trusted friends to monitor the sermons with this concern in mind. It is never easy, but it must be done.

Usually, a pastor is asked to resign on the basis of incompetence, incompatibility, or even heresy. The latter needs careful arbitration by a denominational staff or a council of peers or the Judicatory Ministerial Relations committee. Heresy charges are serious, and if they prove to be unfounded, the pastor's name should be cleared in a formal, public way.

Sexual Misconduct

Moral charges are difficult to handle. In this decade the issues of clergy misconduct have come to the fore in a very public way. Some helpful books for the committee to consider are listed under Appendix A, page 88. A frank discussion of the matter needs to be made by the committee before a pastor comes to the church. Advance preparation will help if your church should ever have to deal with a situation involving clergy sexual misconduct.

Steps the church can take should a minister be accused of such misconduct are:

1. The official board must be made aware of the situation immediately, with the pastor present. Clandestine meetings make for misunderstandings and innuendo. The charges may be unfounded. An occupational hazard of the ministry is that the pastor is vulnerable to charges of apparent moral misbehavior. Pastors must have the right to give their side of the case.

2. The regional minister should be called immediately for counsel and advice. Judicatory persons are well aware of all of the ramifications of the issue. Even though the free church tradition maintains the freedom and autonomy of the church and even though the minister is hired (and fired) by the local church, lawsuits often extend to the larger judicatory of any denomination; therefore, regional ministers must be contacted promptly when a situation has legal considerations.

3. Sometimes it is necessary for the church to find legal counsel because of impending lawsuits from victims in these cases. The best counsel seems to be that if the charges are founded (admittance by the person of wrongdoing), it is best for the church to admit what has happened. Nothing will be gained by denial.

4. While great attention is given to the minister in the case, victims have been desperately hurt. The church must somewhere seek to minister to these persons.

5. Usually a pastor will need to leave if charges of sexual misconduct are founded. The church, in conjunction with the help and advice of the regional minister, should try to help a pastor in this situation. Sometimes it has been possible for forgiving church leaders to keep the penitent pastor on the staff. The situation needs to be carefully weighed. If there is grace for other sins and other people, there is grace for ministers also. But such is not always the general feeling of churches.

6. No public farewell service should be held when a pastor leaves under the duress of sexual misconduct.

A pastor leaving on the basis of morals charges can do a service to the church and the kingdom by writing a letter to the church that admits wrong and asks for forgiveness. This is no attempt to ask to stay but is simply a way of showing that the pastor is conscious of the wrongdoing and, having asked God's forgiveness, now asks for the congregation's forgiveness.

Never is the counsel, concern, kindness, and maturity of the pastoral relations committee more needed (and tested) than in a situation where moral charges are made against the pastor. The name of the church and the concern for righteousness are at stake. But the church needs also to remember that the pastor and the pastor's family need grace and gentleness. "Bear one another's burdens."

The Problem Farewell

When a pastor is forced to resign, an immediate reaction on his or her part is to declare, "I don't want a farewell service. If they have one, I won't show." That is childish, to say the least. This is no time to show such pique. There are people who love the pastor. *They* want a farewell. Furthermore, people of integrity who on an objective basis voted for the pastor's resignation nonetheless respect the pastor and want to do the right thing. The right thing is severance pay and other practicalities. The right thing is also a farewell service (except as noted above). For the church to join ranks in such a meeting also says something to the whole community watching the church. For friends, for the church, for the community, for the cause of Christ (as time will finally tell), it is best for the pastor to stand tall and to accept the farewell service.

Church leaders do well to ask the district denominational office to have a representative there. Not all farewell services can be attended by the staff, but for this farewell staff members will make every effort to be there.

The master of ceremonies will major on the positive aspects of the pastor's ministry. People who have been helped can share a word of witness. Favorite songs, a love offering, and an excellent meal will still be a part of that meeting. The service will be extremely helpful to the pastor's children who have felt hurt because of the pastor's forced resignation.

The Final Farewell—at the Death of a Pastor

When a pastor dies—especially a well-loved one or one with small children—the congregation feels a very deep grief. My wife, Nancy, in her book *Adventure in Dying*, wrote of the church service after the death of her first husband who was the pastor.

That Sunday morning service as a difficult one, I am told. The
church was packed again with people who were hurting deeply. I
suppose in microcosm they had gone through much of my experience—the despair, hope, desperate praying, searching for a word
from God that Lin would be healed, the battering on the doors of
heaven.[16]

In such cases, it will be good for the pastoral relations committee to
be aware that the next pastor will be an interim. Therefore, wise counsel
for the church would be that it seek out an interim who can stay for an
extended time to help the congregation deal adequately with grief.

The funeral service itself becomes a way for the church to join the
family in its grief and to express corporate grief and hope.

There is great value in the funeral service. . . . a "rite" of passage. . . .

It is an acceptable time in which the feelings of grief can be
openly displayed. It is a time in which friends and the community
can come together to share their loss with the bereaved and with
each other. It is a time for an expression of religious faith and in
which those in attendance can offer support and encouragement to
the bereaved. . . .

For me the funeral was a celebration. The name of Christ was
uplifted and hope was given to me, to my boys, and to the believers
assembled there. That is the way it should be.[17]

The church must concern itself with caring for the pastor's spouse and
children. As a practical matter, the church needs to consider a *minimum*
of six months' salary and housing allowance (or the use of the parsonage)
for the family. Never is the church more Christian than in its care of "the
widows and orphans." My wife, Nancy, said that had it not been for the
church caring for her and the children in practical ways, we never would
have made it. With Paul, she could say, "I have been very thoroughly
initiated into the human lot with all its ups and downs. . . . I have strength
for anything through him who gives me power. But it was kind of you to
share the burden of my troubles" (Philippians 4:12-14, NEB). Sharing her
burden meant, to her church, giving financial help, at times providing food
and help with the children, and helping her move to another home.

The Work of the Committee in the Period Between Pastors

4

M ost often, the time between the former pastor's leaving and the new pastor's coming is called the interim period. It has also been referred to as "'Between the No Longer and the Not Yet'' (Wells); . . . 'The In-between times' (Oswald); 'The Period of the Vacant Pulpit' (Mead).''[1]

Most of this language suggests a critical, uneasy time for the church. And it is—the shepherd, the "helmsman," is gone. This is especially crucial when a pastor has left at a critical time in the lives of families of the church: in the midst of marriage counseling, a family member's dying, helping a teenager in his or her struggles; the dependency of older persons, housebound or in nursing homes, upon this pastor's care. We have pointed to the grief that is experienced by the congregation and the panic at the realization that the familiar voice and face are not present any longer.

Often the pastor by the sheer force of his or her charisma has maintained a strong church unity in a church of pluralistic theology, life-styles, and goals for mission. Now the *leader* is no longer here. As an executive minister and interim consultant to many churches, too often I saw the potential for all sorts of self-styled leaders or power blocs to surface in the interim period.

In a time of potential crisis, *communication* is not as regular and clear as it once was. The minister, who (as part of his or her administrative work) saw that regular announcements to the people were made and communications between official boards and committees took place (often through his or her own presence in those meetings), has been replaced by a pulpit supply and volunteer workers. This is especially true in the single-staff church. In these churches no one is working "full time"; no one has the full picture; and people are always asking, "Who knows?"

In large, multiple-staff churches, while assignments for handling pastoral care, administration, and communication can be made by the board, an issue of another sort can arise: because the senior minister, once the "primary among equals," is no longer there to shepherd the staff, infighting, sparring for the position of senior minister, or low morale can easily develop.

The most difficult problem of all may be that the church settles for letting itself remain motionless, like a ship sitting dead in the water, for six to eighteen months. I am convinced that the church, of which Christ said, "The gates of Hell shall not prevail against it," should not settle for anything but to move ahead, even if it is at a reduced speed. A *survival mode* is not where the church should ever be. It is possible for the church to be creative and forward looking and *grow* during the interim period. That is the time for all the gifts to be called forth and used in the unity of the Spirit. In a small church, deacons can make helpful calls and meet with the bereaved as official representatives of the church. It may be *the* opportunity for the doctrine of the priesthood of all believers to be put into concrete action which can forever shape the ministry of that church.

The pastoral relations committee may not have, in its specific list of functions, keeping the ship fueled and moving during the interim period, but it ought to have at least a concern about those functions. If the committee is concerned about pastoral relations, it certainly does have a stake in the relations of the congregation to whatever leadership it chooses to use. My belief is that the church board or diaconate should designate the committee to monitor the climate, work with interim preachers, and so on, and begin work as the core of the pastoral search committee.

"Meanwhile, who fills the pulpit?" is the big question after "When do you think we can get a new minister?"

A Church's Five Alternatives

1. A gifted lay person (or persons) from the church can take the pulpit. I have sometimes seen the diaconate in smaller churches take charge and do a creditable job in caring for the Sunday services.

2. The pulpit can be filled by a changing pulpit supply. Different guest speakers are asked to come each Sunday. This is the least expensive way of having professional speakers but also the least desirable. The church generally gets a hodgepodge of good sermons—but sometimes two speakers may use the same text! The system gives an air of uncertainty to the congregation, especially to those people who are not members. Further, it is a frustrating task for the coordinator of the system. Mix-ups occur. Sometimes two persons show up on the same Sunday or no one shows or someone comes at the wrong hour. The system is only tolerable and demands close coordination between pulpit committee and pulpit supply committee.

Leonard Hill cites an example in which the work of a church in North Carolina suffered from a mix-up:

> The pulpit committee had spent much time in prayer and investigation before deciding that a certain preacher definitely was not the man to serve their church as pastor. Meanwhile the pulpit supply committee . . . asked him to supply one Sunday.
>
> While preaching, the man [revealed his interest] in coming as pastor. . . . church members were so impressed with his sermon delivery that they turned a deaf ear to the pulpit committee's warning that [he] did not always practice as he preached. At the close of the Sunday night service they called him as pastor.
>
> . . . one layman later [said]: "We learned our lesson the hard way." [2]

3. Another possibility is to use constant pulpit supply or an interim preacher. One person is asked to fill the pulpit only. The weakness of such a situation (as in the second alternative) is apparent: the other areas of ministry may suffer. If a church does go the route of pulpit supply, as is the case with many smaller town and country churches, the responsibility of calling and counseling must be assumed by the deacons. Finding time is always a problem for laypersons in ministry but I can cite cases in which laypersons have taken this responsibility and the ministry prospered.

4. A part-time interim pastor can fill the pulpit. Usually this person

serves the church several days a week and commutes to the church. He
or she does all of the preaching, conducts wedding and funeral services,
does visitation, and is available for counseling. His or her time is
limited, but the people know that a pastor is available in time of need.

5. A full-time interim pastor could be used. Retired ministers, denominational personnel, missionaries on furlough, and seminary stu-
dents are people who can be interim pastors of skill and ability and are
able to give time to such a ministry. Having a full-time interim pastor
is generally viewed as the ideal situation. Church work moves forward
and even increases in many instances. For a large church a full-time
interim pastor is a must. For any church which recognizes that there
will be a sizeable interim period, the interim pastor—part-time or full-
time—seems to be the best route.

Considering an Interim Pastor

Lyle Schaller delineates six types of parish situations in which the
concept of an interim pastor merits serious consideration.

1. When the pastor who has served his or her congregation for over
fifteen years dies or retires, an interim of six months to two years is
needed. "In approximately four out of five of such parishes, regardless
of whether the pastor dies or retires after his fifteen or twenty or thirty
or forty years, the next minister is an interim pastor."

2. The second type of parish where an interim pastorate may be
appropriate is closely related to the first: the church whose pastor leaves
after fifteen or twenty years' service. The successor faces more favorable
odds than the successor in the first situation, "but, in a majority of the
cases studied, the next minister also is an interim pastor—though frequently he [she] does not realize it until several years later."

3. Where there has been a strong authoritarian type of leadership (a
type now in sharp decline in terms of popularity!), in order for the new
style of collaborative leadership with a broad base of participation to
come into being, it seems best that an interim pastor follow such a
strong authoritative leader.

4. Following a young pastor who has died, a mature interim pastor
can help the congregation work through its grief and prepare for the
next pastor.

5. Where there has been major internal disturbance in the church—

the church has polarized or gone downhill or the pastor has been asked to leave by reason of heresy, morals or incompetence—a stable, mature interim pastor can help to heal the church and can assist the church in gaining self-confidence and credibility.

6. When a major change is occurring in the community, an interim pastor may be needed to bridge the two eras, e.g. the white congregation in a community into which an increasing number of people from other cultures are moving or the rural church that finds itself now engulfed by the city.

The interim pastor, who has no future with the church, comes only to serve the Lord Jesus Christ. This is usually a person of maturity, and can be used by God to bridge many gaps in order for the permanent pastor to come into a long, happy, fruitful pastorate. The interim pastor should be carefully chosen. It is his or her task to build up. Generally speaking, he/she should not be part of the pastoral selection process nor should the interim pastor attend the meetings of the pulpit committee.[3]

The amount to pay the full-time interim pastor has many variables: what he or she may be asking; the experience, skill, training he or she has; the size of the church's budget. I agree with Dr. Fred Prinzing that an interim "should receive the same salary, minus fringe benefits, which the previous pastor received. (Some judicatories recommend two-thirds of the base amount.)"[4] A part-time interim might "receive double what a pulpit supply [speaker] receives [plus travel expenses]. Another formula which has been used satisfactorily is to give the part time interim pastor each Sunday one percent of the previous pastor's base salary. . . ."[5]

Special Skills an Interim Pastor Brings

1. A "vision" of what that church can do. By giving a certain stability ("someone is steering the thing again"), the interim can provide a positive up-beat attitude of what can be done in the period between pastors.

2. The skill of dealing with issues in a pastoral way while at the same time being neutral (he or she has no future, no ax to grind) is invaluable for the church that is now so unsettled.

3. Healing rifts, settling issues, and being the person who "weans"

the congregation from the former pastor and readies the church to receive the new shepherd.

4. The interim pastor can remind the people—and model it—that as they look for a new pastor, they are still people with a mission.

5. New models for ministry and life together can be shown, helping the people to be able to break free of a certain style.[6]

Perhaps Philip Porcher's words best declare the possibilities of the "period in-between:"

> I have a fantasy of a congregation moving through the months of the interim period. A group of people are walking slowly ahead, often looking backward with longing and lost expressions on their faces. Gradually, they begin to look at each other, some in anger and frustration, others in supportive collaboration, and still others in small groups pulling off to the side. Then, as weeks and months go by, they continue to move ahead but now more as a unified group, looking ahead with expressions of hope and eager anticipation on their faces.[7]

Procedures in Calling a Pastor

5

In most churches with a congregational polity, the bylaws call for a pastoral search committee, which is truly representative of the church, to be formed, to seek a new pastor. True representation is commendable. The pastor is pastor of the whole church. Each segment needs the opportunity to share in the choice of pastor and in the search and selection process.

Because representation seems to be the basic qualification for service on the committee, other important factors are sometimes forgotten, such as the committee's needs for definite understanding of the role of pastoral leadership and clear knowledge of the congregation's strengths and weaknesses. The members of the pastoral relations committee are persons who, if they have served well, understand these two areas more clearly than anyone else. Further, as I have already indicated, there is much need for a continuity of relationship from the original negotiations with the pastoral candidate to his or her ministry as pastor of the church. A possible weak link in the system is that quite often the pastoral search committee concludes its work and a new group of people on the pastoral relations committee begins working with the minister.

To avoid the lack of continuity, it seems most sensible that the pastoral relations committee be the *core* of a pastoral search committee. Most pastoral search committees have from five to nine members. If additional representative people were added to the three- to five-member pastoral relations committee, the process of calling a pastor would be immeasurably strengthened. Church bylaws could read: "When the congregation votes to form a pastoral search committee, current membership of the pastoral relations committee shall be part of that committee, as voting members." While this chapter can be a guide for the pastoral search committee, it is contained in this book so that the pastoral relations committee can have full understanding of the ethos and ethics of the initial process and negotiations of calling a pastor.

The process seems to divide itself into seven phases.

Phase 1: Organizing the Committee

Most churches realize the necessity and importance of establishing a committee for calling a pastor. The process is so involved and time consuming that the entire congregation cannot act as a committee. Therefore, it delegates to a committee that task. No more delicate operation, demanding more commitment and leading of the Holy Spirit, exists within the church than the work of the pastoral search committee. The name of the committee varies. "Call Committee" and "Pulpit Committee" have time-bound tradition behind them. Some persons take issue with the latter term since the task at hand is more than just locating an outstanding pulpiteer. Garland Hendricks therefore opts for "Pastoral Selection Committee."[1] That may seem to be giving more authority to the committee than the free church tradition wants; so the term "pastor search committee" may be useful.[2]

Qualifications of a Committee Member

A committee member should be, above all, a person of spiritual maturity. The task of choosing a pastor under our congregational system demands a high level of spiritual maturity. Second, he or she must have the respect of the congregation. This may be already apparent because of the offices he or she already holds. The need for credibility is self-evident in a system which allows a few to speak for the whole. Third, anyone who accepts the appointment should be committed to give the time and devotion required in the performance of the task. Make no mistake about it, a great amount of time is required to do the job well. Fourth, the potential committee person should know the church well—its needs, strengths, weaknesses, aspirations, and so on.

Officers of the Committee

Unless the chairperson is designated ahead of time, the first task of the committee is to elect one. To facilitate this, it is wise to ask the vice-chairperson of the church or chairperson of the diaconate (or church board) to convene the meeting. The burden of responsibility falls heavily upon the shoulders of the chairperson. He or she must possess qualities of leadership, a sensitive spirit, and an ability and drive to get things done. A vice-chairperson is selected and made responsible for acting in the absence of the chairperson or on instruction of the committee. A secretary is selected and instructed to make and preserve records of meetings, discussions, decisions, reports, and recommendations. All return correspondence from a candidate should be directed to the secretary's home.

Clarifying the Committee's Role

Details of the committee's role cannot be listed in the bylaws. If the details are not in some approved manual of operation, the committee needs formal approval by the church board and/or the church of its specific role. Understandings in six areas need to be reached:

1. Is the committee responsible for obtaining pulpit supply and/or an interim pastor?

2. How much is the committee expected to do toward securing a pastor? For instance, is it simply to locate men and women to preach before the church, or is it to do whatever is necessary until it is ready to recommend one choice for pastor?

3. Concerning such things as salary, housing, business expenses, fringe benefits, moving expenses, vacation, continuing education, time for denominational work, and so on—how much is to be determined by board action or church action and how much is to be left to the discretion of the committee? Is this to be decided before the search for a pastor begins, or is the committee expected to make recommendations about such matters to the church (or appropriate board) at whatever time seems best?

4. Has the church outlined some basic qualifications a prospective pastor must have, or is this to be left entirely to the wisdom of the committee?

5. How much money will the church provide for pulpit committee

expense? What kind of accounting for expense funds is expected of the committee?

6. Is there a limit on the amount of time the committee will have to do its work?[3]

Agreeing on Procedure

Begin work as soon as the committee is established. Since the work will often take four to six months, it is important to begin immediately. There is sometimes a queasiness about beginning the search for a new pastor while the pastor is still on the field—especially if he or she is well liked. A pastor who cares about the ministry of the church will not object if the church moves ahead to find his or her successor. Under normal circumstances to delay work until the pastor has left the field is to delay unnecessarily.

Before any work begins, the committee must become a single working unit through a period of sharing, Scripture reading, and prayer together. Members must get used to one another and covenant to work together. They are going to be together a great deal. Ken McQuere observes: "The constitution cannot give to the committee one needed ingredient— unity. The members should come together as a team without any superstars wanting to make all the decisions."[4] Sometimes a retreat for several days can accomplish this sense of "team." Taking time at each meeting to "get on board" with one another is important.

Agree together to keep reports and files on pastors and churches confidential. Many pastors have had their reputations tarnished by the airing of confidential reports about them—true or not. Sometimes when a person's name is mentioned as being under consideration, the news has filtered back to his or her own church and his or her people jump to the conclusion that he or she wants to leave. That person is then caught in the bind of all that this news implies. Keep confidential the names being considered.

Review your constitution and bylaws for any specific procedures that are demanded, e.g., the length of advance notice to the congregation on the coming of a candidate and the calling of the pastor, and the percentage of vote that is needed for a call, and so on. This will avoid embarrassment and parliamentary logjams later on.

Make the pastoral search committee's recommendation of a candidate unanimous. For a person to come to the pastorate with one or more members of the search committee in opposition to his or her coming is to lay the foundation for dissension.

Plan periodic reports to the congregation. Because one of the problems in the interim between pastors is the seeming silence of the pastoral search committee, it is important that the chairperson periodically *assures* the church of the committee's hard work and, at the same time, asks for prayer support. Announcements in the bulletin and church paper of pastoral search committee meetings assure the church that the committee has not given up. A letter to the congregation at the onset of the committee's work, enunciating the procedures, would be helpful (See Appendix D).

If it is not set forth in the bylaws or in the church's instructions to the committee, then the decision to present one name only should be agreed upon by committee members. (This does not mean that in the early stages of the work several prospects will not be examined.) There are two reasons for this. First, persons are not measured against one another, but against a common standard. Second, it aids harmony and unity within the church so that some factions in the church will not be desiring one person, the rest another.

If a church and committee do decide to have more than one person candidate before the vote to call is taken, each candidate should be informed of the procedure. Very few persons will enter the lists!

The rest of this chapter outlines suggested specific procedures for a committee's work. Review them and agree upon *(a)* the steps to be taken, *(b)* the information of the church and its ministry that the committee will prepare, and *(c)* what will be expected from each candidate.

Calling the Denominational Office

A church that is a member of a denomination can avail itself of the best help possible by calling the denominational office and asking for a staff person in charge of counseling search committees and conducting pastoral placement to meet with the committee at its first meeting. The usual procedure is for the church moderator to notify the denominational office of a pastoral vacancy. The office then takes the initiative to offer its services. The skills and knowledge of the denominational staff person will help the committee work through its process, a task for which the members have little experience and which is largely a one-time experience. Further, the denomination has the whole picture of the situation and can supply names of likely candidates. Finally, the denomination is concerned about the welfare and mission of *this* church and is dedicated to seeking adequate pastoral leadership for it.

(Ultimately, however, it must be noted that the value of the denominational staff input is dependent entirely on the attitude and style by which that staff person approaches the church. If it is in genuine collegiality, help is accepted. Pontificated directives are seen as just that and are usually rejected out of hand.)

Tempering the Interim Period

In the last chapter we discussed the need and value of an interim pastor. While it may be that the diaconate has responsibility for interim pastoral leadership, the search committee should not allow itself to be pressured to make supply pastors, interim pastors, or speakers candidates for the vacancy. The whole process of an impartial, unpressured selection can be easily short-circuited when an interim speaker is suddenly championed as a candidate. *Seldom* have I seen that laying aside agreed-upon procedures resulted in a happy selection of a pastor.

Phase 2: Profile of the Pastor

From various sources the committee proceeds to draw up a profile of standards for the pastor.

Scriptural Qualifications

The New Testament records qualifications for a pastor in 1 Timothy 3:1-7 and Titus 1:6-9. The passages teach that a pastor ought to have a good reputation in three circles of life: in the church, in society, and in his or her own home. From a *negative* viewpoint he or she is *not* to be self-pleasing, quick-tempered, or given to wine or money. From a *positive* viewpoint he or she *is* to love people, love God, and be sensible, mature, and Christlike. From a *professional* viewpoint he or she *is* to be able to teach, be able to manage, and be a sound theologian.

It appears that these qualifications are to be sought in any pastor the church chooses. They represent the common factors desired in any pastor regardless of the other skills, training, abilities, and gifts one may look for to meet the special needs of the congregation.

Church and Community Profile

It seems apparent that before the pastoral search committee can determine the kind of person it is searching for, it needs to do some investigation and give thought to self-understanding and to put this self-understanding down on paper in what we call a "church profile." This profile can then serve another function.

Given to a prospective candidate, the profile provides him or her with a full picture of the church and its ministry in the community so that, though not having visited the church, he or she can make a decision as to whether his or her gifts could be used in that situation at all.

To help the committee honestly assess its church and community, the information suggested under Appendix E ought to be supplied. This information should be duplicated and pictures of the church and parsonage (and perhaps material from the area chamber of commerce) put together in a folder in order for enough copies to be available for prospective candidates and for the district office.

The whole process finally gives valuable input to the candidate profile.

The Congregational Input

Additional help for the committee's formulation of the pastor's profile can be gained by asking the congregation to respond to a questionnaire on a Sunday morning. Using the questionnaire is not an absolute necessity but it does serve two functions. It gives a broad view of the kind of person the people prefer and it gives them an opportunity to become part of the process. A criticism often leveled against pastoral search committees is that they are "doing it all by themselves."

A sample questionnaire is to be found in Appendix F. Some factors to be kept in mind during the presentation of the questionnaire are the following:

Take time *during* the morning service to fill it out. The pastoral search committee chairperson should present it and give instructions.

The questionnaire should be filled out anonymously.

All regular attenders as well as members should be given the opportunity to fill it out. They should check a box indicating whether they are members or only attenders.

The papers should be collected during the service (if they are taken home, you may have only a 30 percent response).

It must be borne in mind that the response to the questionnaire will be somewhat predictable. Naturally all members want youth, experience, successful past pastorates, well-trained, excellent speakers with charming spouses! That is generally what you will find out. Nonetheless, the input is valuable; the congregation has become part of the process.

The Shape of the Pastor's Profile

Taking the profile of church and community (which, it is hoped, will spell out some of the specific qualities you will be looking for in the new pastor) plus congregational input, the pulpit committee must then *prayerfully* set up its profile of the person they will look for.

Somewhere in the process of determining the kind of pastor that should be called, the committee ought to set priorities on the kinds of ministries it would like him or her to perform—in short, to set priorities for his or her time. Then, when interviewing a candidate, the committee can respond intelligently to the question he or she may ask: "What do you want of your pastor?" all recognizing that there is always too much to do.

Again, Lyle Schaller provides an interesting way for a committee to arrive at consensus as regards pastoral expectations. He divides the function of the minister into twelve categories:

Visiting
Teaching
Counseling
Administration
Evangelism
Leader among leaders
Community leader
Enabler
Leading worship and preaching
Denominational responsibilities
Personal and spiritual growth
The leader of the church[5]

Appendix G shows how these twelve areas (you may wish to delete some) can be put on cards, each committee member arranging them in order of lowest and highest priorities. This will provide an excellent additional input into the profile of the person you are looking for.

Special Considerations

In devising the profile, the committee should be mindful of two special concerns.

The Single Pastor

Increasingly we are seeing more single persons at seminary. They are part of a youth culture that puts less premium on being married. These single men and women sense God's call to service. They have gifts and do not feel that they are missing out on "God's best" by being unmarried. They should be considered equally with their married peers.

The single pastor has strengths that should be carefully weighed. Like Paul, he or she is not caught up with all of the concerns of family life. The church is his or her family and the single pastor can give himself or herself to its nourishing. While a married pastor has insights into certain aspects of family living, it must also be said that the single status provides special insights and understandings of a whole segment of the church. My own personal feeling about single pastors is that generally they quickly sense when people are hurting and move to heal those hurts in a compassionate way. No church should rule out a candidate for the sole reason that he or she is single.

The Pastor's Spouse

The pastoral search committee should and does have a definite interest in the pastor's spouse. Too often pastors' wives have been seen as unpaid assistants or free church secretaries or organists. A new set of dynamics is involved with pastors' husbands. A new phenomenon is the church's task of welcoming Rev. and Mr. _____ to the church!

Some women clergy are married to men who are pastors in other churches. This situation has a whole set of dynamics that must be carefully understood and covenanted for by the church which calls a woman as pastor. The traditional expectations simply do not fit. The male spouse who is pastor of another church has another whole arena of ministry and role expectations. In one sense, it is not unlike dealing with a pastor who is unmarried. This may be an opportunity for the church to deal with the expectations they place on the male *or* female spouse.

Some pastors come with their pastor-spouses as a team. In many ways, the co-pastor couple is an easier entity to covenant with since the two pastors are in the family *and* the same team. Important matters to consider in such a situation are confidentiality in counseling and the potential for polarization of the couple as church members may try to play one off the other.

A different set of dynamics exists where the woman pastor is married to a man who is not a pastor. There are definite adjustments for that male spouse. One female pastor has said that there is great potential for stress because the wife's work demands not only long hours of work but also "prime time" evening hours. (This is not unlike the pastor's wife's criticism of the "schedule".) Emergency calls in the middle of the night can be difficult for the male spouse, says another female pastor, especially if there are small children in the house. Also the male spouse may get tired of attending meetings with his pastor-wife, though the expectations of him by the church are not the same as those of a pastor's wife—so far.

One of the important adjustments for both spouses in this relationship is that most people are mystified by it all and have no easy ways of handling "Rev. and Mr. _____" (except perhaps to joke about it!). Breaking the ice for a new role is never easy.

Important questions to consider when a pastor has responded to a call to a church and the spouse has joined the pastor are: Was he or she clearly a part of that decision? Can he or she find the kind of job he or she wants? If the pastor is a woman, will the marriage be a role reversal of the traditional model, where, in fact, the husband may take care of the home, not working outside? If in years to come the pastor receives a "call" to another church, will the spouse be willing to leave his or her position and go? These are questions that the clergy couple should have worked out before accepting the call to a church.

The views of the pastor's spouse are of great importance. The two important questions the search committee needs to satisfy itself with are whether or not the spouse is happy with the role of *pastor's spouse* and all its implications, and, is the spouse happy that his or her mate has accepted the call of the ministry?[6]

Phase 3: Nominations for the Pastorate

The committee now moves to the important task of securing names of persons to be considered.

Securing Names

Names can come, solicited or unsolicited, from many sources: friends of the church; members of the church; seminary placement offices; persons who volunteer themselves; and, very importantly, through the denominational region office.

Most national bodies maintain a file on their clergy. Important information regarding those persons is available, and now, increasingly through the use of a computer, this information comes in print-out form. The computer profile system, cursed by some pastors who feel they are somehow at the mercy of a computer (which is not true—though they may be at the mercy of regional ministers who use a computer), nevertheless allows a California church to know about and consider a pastor in Maine. Among American Baptist churches, for instance, the denomination's American Baptist Personnel Services "data indicate that 95 percent of pulpit committees use the system and 90 percent find the person hired for a vacancy through the system and profile. The system, therefore, appears to have a high level of acceptance as a useful information source."[7]

The entire church membership should be allowed to nominate candidates. It can be announced that the pulpit committee is glad to receive nominations for candidates. This will be enough. Interested people will search for names and write to the chairperson to share a name. It is counterproductive to ask, at the same time the congregational questionnaire is handed out, that people propose candidates (you will get some through this process anyway). People will feel *obligated* to put *some* name down and you as a committee may be obliged to search through eighty names!

The committee should ask, in fact, demand that the name of the person submitting a name also be given, that the proposal be in writing, and that at least one good reason be given why the committee should consider the person. As much information as possible should be provided about the candidate. I say this after seeing pulpit committees faithfully struggle to get information about almost unknown (and often unqualified) candidates.

The submission of names should not be regarded as a straw vote. Simply because five different people give the same name may mean only that one family likes the candidate. Accept the names graciously, but do not be intimidated by what sometimes can be politicking.

Recommendations

No person should be considered as a candidate without good recommendations; recommendations should be made by persons whose integrity and judgment can be trusted and who have had close contact with the candidate recently. The ideal recommendation will reveal weaknesses as well as strengths and will explain why the recommender feels the person is suited to the church.

As names, which are totally unknown to the committee, come to the committee, it may be well to check with the denominational office and ask the placement staff person for a frank evaluation. Further information can be obtained by writing to the regional executive in whose region the person has served. In some search process/placement systems a regional minister will respond only to requests for recommendations from another regional office.

At this point, if the committee is wrestling with fifty names, it is not possible to follow up every recommendation in an in-depth way. After the list has been narrowed, a more rigorous attempt to learn more about a candidate can be made.

Narrowing the List

The maximum number of candidates the committee should deal with at any given time is six. Begin by taking the profile of the pastor that the committee developed in Phase 2. Try to measure the persons on the list against that standard. Fully half of the candidates will immediately be put aside. The committee will be most concerned about the people on the rest of the list. The inquiries and questionnaires will prove helpful in working with these candidates.

Prayerfully review each candidate, weighing the recommendations. A valuable exercise is to let each committee member rank the top three candidates against the profile that has been set. Having completed the ranking, let each member indicate why he or she ranked the candidates this way. The top six people will form *the list of candidates*.

Phase 4: Choosing the Candidate

There are three steps in this phase, each one demanding increasing thoroughness.

Write to the Top Nominees

Up to this time in the process the committee has not directly contacted any of the persons on its list. There are ethics involved here. For the committee to write to everyone on the list—perhaps twenty people—and seek to determine their concern and yet not indicate each person's eligibility (at best only one-twentieth!) is, I feel, unfair. It would needlessly raise the hopes of some. It wastes the time of many. One church sent out "job applications" to one hundred persons. Needless to say, when pastors realized that it was a mass mailing, very few applied.

Write to the top six (or less) nominees to determine their willingness to have their names stand as candidates. (Some churches prefer to make a phone call prior to sending a letter.) The danger is that the candidate may say "not interested" on the basis of insufficient information. Giving full information is best, imparted in the following manner.

Type a separate letter to each candidate. A *sample* of the style and content of such a letter is found in Appendix I. Do not send a mimeographed letter.

Include the profile of the church (which ought also to include an attractive color photo of the church and parsonage).

Include a copy of the church's constitution and bylaws (if these are very old and about to be amended, you may note what changes are in the offing).

Usually it is wise *not* to include a copy of the annual report. The report contains the figures for salaries and other costs for pastoral remuneration. These should be negotiable with a candidate. If the person that you want sees a very low salary, he or she may turn the church down at this juncture, feeling that the Lord would not move him or her to a substantial cut in his or her present salary.

Do not send a questionnaire. I always felt, when a questionnaire accompained the initial inquiry, that I was being asked to apply for the job! This is not the case. There is a world of difference between you, as a committee representing the church, asking a person to consider being a candidate and that person applying for the position. Time will come later for candidates to fill out a questionnaire.

Remember, the warmth of your letter, its neatness, and style are all the reader has by which to judge your church at this point. It is your first overture to him or her as a potential candidate. Make it do its work!

Ask for a reply by a certain date, preferably within two weeks. If a candidate writes and asks for more time, allow 'it. If you receive no answer within two weeks and if you feel this person to be an excellent choice, you may want to call, asking if any further information might help.

As the replies come in, you will find that generally about one-half of the persons answer saying that they are interested in letting their names stand as candidates. The final list of candidates should seldom have more than three names.

Visit the Candidates

Make plans to visit each candidate in his or her home church. (For special cases in which this cannot be done because a person is not a pastor of a church, see the next section.) Preferably, the entire committee should make the visit. If distance may prevent the whole group's going, then those who go should make careful notes so that an accurate reporting of facts and impressions can be made to the full committee.

Call the candidate and mutually arrange a date to visit the church to hear him or her speak and to visit with him or her after the service. The day of sneaking into a church, collars up, dark glasses on, and spreading through the congregation is over. Make the date. He or she already knows of your interest, you of his or hers. Surely the pastor will do his or her very best that Sunday, but who wants to hear someone at the worst? Besides, committees who have come unannounced have often found a missionary speaker in the pulpit!

The function of the visit is to determine the kind of preacher he or she is *and* to interview him or her and to share in detail the ministry of your church. Therefore, invite him or her (and his or her spouse—not family) out to dinner at the time you make the appointment for your visit. Not to make such an arrangement in advance is to risk accomplishing only half of your mission—hearing the person preach. He or she may have an appointment for dinner by the time you make the invitation at the church door after the service.

When you make a visit, there is a certain pastoral search committee etiquette to follow. While you do not sneak into church, neither is it necessary to march in and take up the two front pews. Enter into the spirit of the whole service. You are there to listen and to be part of the congregation. If people ask where you are from, don't lie.

In the worship service look for such things as orderliness of service, unique or creative parts, participation of the people, the general mood of the congregation, attentiveness to the sermon, what the pastor says in his or her message; notice his or her voice and sincerity.

The interview that follows the service is as important as hearing the person. The interview should perhaps begin with a statement of the candidate's personal walk with God and his or her general family background. Typical interview questions will also include what the candidate (and his or her family) does for recreation, what he or she hopes to be doing a decade from now, the last six books he or she has read, what the candidate's continuing education program is, what the candidate's view is of the church today, what his or her frustrations are about the ministry, what he or she likes to do best, what he or she is best at, what are his or her experiences in evangelism, ideas about worship, attitudes toward missions and toward the denomination, views on stewardship, health, cooperation with other churches, participation in community programs and service organizations, way of working with staff (volunteer and paid), view of and participation in Christian education, and understanding of his or her faith and life-style. Somewhere the common discussion ought to arrive at an open view of what the committee's church is like and what the church sees as its future and hence is seeking in the pastor it is calling.

The interview should continue long enough so that the candidate and committee can satisfy themselves that they know each other well. The

committee should be prepared to talk in a preliminary way—if the
pastor should ask—of policies of the church, remuneration, vacation,
and other benefits. The committee should have reached some understandings with the church on what can be offered to the candidate before
this phase of the process. The pastoral search committee should be
allowed the privilege to negotiate. In matters of salary, some churches
have allowed the committee a high and low range in which the committee
can negotiate, dependent upon the experience and training the person
would bring to the job. Generally at this point in the talks, ball park
figures are used. When and if he or she visits the church as candidate,
the figures should be exact.

If the interview has gone well, the final question might well be:
"How interested are you in becoming pastor of our church?" After
hearing the answer (sometimes fogged in a bit by the usual "Well, we
are very happy here and the Lord is blessing," or "It would really
have to take a direct call from the Lord"), then the committee will get
a feeling whether the candidate ought to remain on its list or not.
Describe the process which your committee is using and say that if he
or she is chosen as the primary candidate, he or she will likely be
called. Again, make it clear that if he or she is asked to candidate and
accepts, that is a sign to you that he or she is *very open* to the call.

On the way home discuss the conversation (need I suggest it?) and
write down impressions while they are still fresh in your minds.

Special Cases

The seminary student obviously has no pulpit. It may be possible for
the seminary placement office or the regional executive to arrange for
the seminarian to preach in a neighboring church as pulpit supply. The
committee can hear him or her there and conduct an interview. Though
not ideal, a cassette tape of a sermon delivered to a real congregation
might be sent to the committee. On occasion, even when planning to
consider more than one seminarian, a church has asked the person to
be pulpit supply. At that point, as far as the public announcement is
made, the seminarian is the pulpit supply during the interim. After the
pulpit committee has heard him or her, it may then decide to interview
and have the person candidate officially in the same process used with
other candidates. It must be remembered, of course, that a seminarian

has little or no track record and that therefore the committee must be more dependent upon the recommendation of the seminary or upon those who know him or her best.

The former missionary, pastor without a church, denominational leader, evangelist, chaplain, and others also lack a regular pulpit in which to preach. The "borrowed pulpit" again is in order. But these persons have track records, and more service information is available about them than is available for the seminarian. Again, generally speaking, these persons have been heard by the church and their ability to preach—or lack of it—is known. The need to hear them prior to a call to candidate is not as acute. The recommendations regarding them should perhaps be more numerous, the personal questionnaire studied more carefully, and the interview more extended.

Quite often in the two special cases mentioned and even for the nominee who cannot quite make up his or her mind to respond to the initial letter asking his or her name to stand as candidate, his or her visit to the field as a *noncandidate* is in order. In this event he or she does not attend a congregational meeting and certainly does not preach, but simply views the area and meets with the pulpit committee.

Finding the Candidate

The awful burden of responsibility that a pastoral search pulpit committee bears is now felt keenly as the procedure demands that out of several possibilities *one person* be chosen as the candidate, to visit the church, preach, meet the people and subsequently be voted upon by the congregation.

The procedure for this committee meeting is simple but important.

1. Time should be spent at the meeting for prayer. It might be helpful to announce to the congregation that the committee will meet that week to make its final choice and ask for prayer on its behalf.

2. Complete profiles should be prepared on all the candidates and should contain material from denominational headquarters, including recommendations, a resumé of recommendations from other sources, and notes of the committee's visit with the candidate.

3. Before any discussion on the merits of the candidate is made, it might be helpful for each committee member independently to rank the candidates.

4. Following the ranking, as the member announces his or her first choice, reasons should be given why he or she has so chosen.

5. It often happens that the ranking is unanimous. The task is then complete. If the ranking is not unanimous, the committee must move to agree on one candidate for presentation to the church. It is well to remember that none are ideal but that the charge to the committee is clear: "Select the candidate who comes closest to meeting your qualifications and make a firm decision regarding his/her candidacy."

Phase 5: The Process of Candidating

Both the candidate and your own church need to be informed of the committee's selection and the date of the candidate's visit to your church.

Notification of the Candidate's Visit

Call the candidate to tell him or her that the committee has chosen him or her as the candidate. Mutually determine a weekend for the candidate (and his or her spouse) to be with the church. Confirm the phone call with a letter listing the date and time of services, indicating the program for the weekend and what is expected from him or her, sending plane or train tickets for him or her and spouse, advising the candidate that the church will cover all expenses, telling him or her where to meet whoever will meet the couple when they arrive.

Send a letter to the congregation indicating the fact of the person's coming and saying that this person is the primary candidate whom the committee is now considering (see Appendix J). Announce the occasion in the bulletin and from the pulpit. Don't surprise the people. They tend to vote down surprises!

Details to Care For

Prepare the way well for the candidate's coming. Remember, at this stage you want the person. Your job is to make the stay a pleasant one. Here are some things the committee should do to insure a smooth stay.

1. Have one couple, preferably the committee chairperson and his or her spouse, host the candidate (i.e., serve as guides and arrangers of details and personal needs).

2. Arrange the motel or hotel accommodations. A private home is

not an ideal place to stay. The candidate and his or her spouse need privacy at this important juncture in their lives.

3. Plan for meals. Some of these may be eaten in church members' homes, but there should be a minimum of these.

4. Arrange for any meetings with boards, committees, or special groups of the church.

5. Alert the social committee if you plan a buffet lunch on Saturday or Sunday evening.

6. Ask the treasurer to have a check ready to give to the candidate before he or she returns home. The church is responsible for paying the candidate's (and spouse's) transportation, lodging, meals (including those purchased when traveling), and an honorarium.

The committee by this time should have a clear understanding with other committees or boards responsible for salary, work schedule, vacation time, and so on as to what can be offered. Plans should be made for a meeting with the boards so that these details can be discussed and negotiated with openness and candor. An understanding, subject to final approval by the church, should be worked out for the following matters: salary; automobile allowance; housing and utilities; book allowance; continuing education fund; hospitality allowance; denominational pension program; major medical and hospitalization and life insurance; sick leave (disability income); conference expenses; moving expenses; any improvements or decorating (home and office) being done before his/her moving; number of people on the church staff and their relationship to the pastor; time allowed for secular work (if part-time work is necessary); time for continuing education (study leaves or sabbaticals); time for special meetings, camps, and similar engagements; vacation time; how supply preachers are to be selected and paid and so on.

The church is a spiritual ministry but it works with dollars and hours, and these need to be contracted for in a forthright and open fashion. The more these are agreed upon in advance of the person's coming, the less chance there will be for conflict later.

The Program for the Weekend

From the time the chairperson meets the candidate and his or her spouse until the time they leave, the pace is set by the chairperson. It is up to him or her to move the schedule along, at the same time being sensitive to the human needs of the candidate and spouse. The following schedule is suggested:

1. If at all possible—especially for a larger church—the candidate and spouse should arrive on Friday afternoon and go directly to the motel. Depending on the arrival time, a meal with the chairpersons of the committee and the church board or deacon board (and spouses) should be arranged—an easy evening of relaxation.

2. Saturday can be given over to driving through the area, viewing the church, parsonage, and schools. If the candidate, by reason of distance, cannot easily return to the area, it might be well to encourage him or her to review the possible decorating program for the parsonage. A trustee committee should meet with the couple at that point. If a house is to be purchased, a review of the neighborhoods, types of houses available, and so on, should be made with the appropriate persons.

3. A buffet supper at church with the leadership or at a restaurant is the order for Saturday evening. At this time it would be helpful for the candidate to meet with the board or committee prepared to discuss remuneration and employment policies. The meeting should not last past 10 P.M. The next day is a big day for the candidate.

4. While the candidate may visit the Sunday church school classes, he or she should not be asked to speak or teach.

5. The morning service should be led by the chairperson of the church board and the candidate asked only to give the Scripture lesson, pastoral prayer, and the sermon—or only the sermon.

6. Many rural churches have begun the lovely custom of having noon dinner at church for the candidate and the whole church family. The opportunity is given for all to meet the candidate and his or her spouse. A time for questions should be given, with the chairperson of the committee fielding them.

7. Still other churches plan an evening buffet to which all officers, board and committee members and spouses are invited at 5 P.M. Time for questions is allowed.

8. It is not necessary that the candidate speak at the Sunday evening service, if the church has one, though many churches so prefer. Sometimes a concert is presented by the choir, and the candidate appears on the program briefly to pray. It often seems the case that it is hard for

the preacher to do well in the evening service. I suspect plain emotional fatigue may have something to do with it.

One of two events may follow the evening service. For the church that had an evening buffet for leaders only, a coffee fellowship can be held so that all people can greet the couple. No question-and-answer time is held now. Or, if time for frank and open discussion *with the board* has not been found, this is the time for it. Some churches will conduct a business meeting after the service and right on the spot vote on the candidate.

Phase 6: Extending the Call

The pastoral search committee and, hence, the whole church is ready to make its decision about the candidate.

The Committee Meeting

Following the candidate's visit, the committee should meet to make final recommendations to the church regarding the candidate. (If the church is to vote that very evening, the committee should briefly meet in the afternoon.) Naturally the committee is committed to calling him or her or it would not have asked him or her to candidate. But sometimes a committee senses a totally negative church response or, upon further knowledge of the person and reflection upon it, decides that it cannot recommend him or her. In that remote event, this decision should be made known to the church either at the business meeting or by special letter, and *his or her name should not come up for vote.* The candidate should be notified *immediately.* This is a matter of ethics. If the committee pulls out its support of the candidate, he or she should not have to face the further ignominy of being voted down by the church.

Remember that proper notification, according to the church's constitution and bylaws, must be made concerning the upcoming business meeting usually called especially for the purpose of calling the pastor.

The Business Meeting

The recommendation to call should be put in writing for two reasons. First, since the terms of the call are to be part of the recommendation, it is important that none of the terms are left out or changed. Second, since the exact wording of the terms must be entered into the minutes of the business meeting, a copy must be given to the church clerk.

A full and open discussion of the terms of the call should be made in the business meeting. The terms are two-fold: policies and remuneration. (See "Compensation Review" in chapter 2.)

Policies

It would be well to include an agreement that the deacon board or church board will meet with the pastor six months after his or her arrival to discuss (a) his or her performance over against congregational expectations and (b) his or her expectations of the church. A further statement would be in order that there be a yearly meeting with just such an agenda.

The amount of time allowed for continuing education should be given. At least a week a year (two weeks preferably) with the right to accumulate two years' time is fair. It must be seen that the value of the special study time accrues to the church. Some churches wisely consider three months' study leave for the pastor.

If the pastor is allowed to work in a secular position (as is sometimes necessary in some small churches), this stipulation should be spelled out clearly.

Most pastors are given some time for special preaching missions— a minimum of one week per year. One week on the staff of a regional camp ought to be allowed also. Both of these last considerations ought to be seen as necessary ministry to the church at large.

Vacation time of at least three weeks *in addition* to the above opportunities should be provided.

Supply preachers should be paid by the church except in cases in which the pastor conducts a preaching mission.

Provisions made yearly for attendance at denominational conferences should be clearly stated. Expenses borne by the church for these functions must also be spelled out.

Moving expenses, including the cost of loading and hauling the furniture plus travel expenses incurred by the pastor and family as they come to the new field, are costs to be paid by the church.

Most churches are gracious and continue to pay a pastor if he or she is ill, in the clear recognition that he or she usually works six days a week and is always on call. Still, some provisions for long-term sick leave might well be written into the agreement of the letter of call.

The Vote

At the business meeting, after the presentation of the candidate and his or her background and qualifications, the motion is made by the pastoral search committee chairperson that the church call the candidate as pastor (usually for an indefinite length of time) on the terms stated. The vote should be by secret ballot and the percentage of vote necessary to call the candidate should be announced. If the vote is sufficient to call the candidate but not unanimous, someone may move that it may be made unanimous. If the candidate wants to know the outcome of the first vote, let him or her know.

Upon the favorable vote of the congregation, an official letter of call should be sent to the candidate stating *all terms*. The letter should be drafted the same day that the business meeting is held. (Courtesy requires a phone call to the pastor-elect after the meeting, telling him or her of the call and indicating that a letter will follow.) See Appendix K for a sample letter of call. *The letter is in fact a legal contract.*

In the event that the church does not vote to call the candidate, courtesy demands an immediate letter to the candidate, thanking him or her for taking time to make the consideration.

In the event of a negative vote on the part of either the church or the candidate, the committee should follow through on the next candidate on its list in the same manner.

Phase 7: The Pastor Arrives

Upon hearing a positive reply from the candidate, the pastoral search committee holds its final meeting.

Checklist Items to Be Reviewed

1. Plans should be made for the installation service (see Appendix L for suggested format). If this becomes the task of the board, the pastoral search committee should have some relationship to those plans.

2. A report of the candidate's acceptance should be made formally to the church.

3. *Letters of notification should be sent to the regional and national denominational offices* so that files will be up to date.

4. Pictures and a news story should be provided for the local newspaper. Generally the newspaper will carry its full story on the first Sunday the pastor preaches.

5. Destroy or return all confidential papers concerning prospective candidates.

6. Send a thank-you letter to each of the persons who were nominees for the candidacy. This will also serve to notify them that they are no longer under consideration. Christian courtesy demands this; yet many churches neglect it. Please be gracious!

7. A brief summary report of the committee's work should be submitted for inclusion in the church clerk's records.

8. A full accounting of the committee's expenses should be presented to the treasurer and any unpaid bills should be presented for payment.

9. With the final report to the church, the committee should be formally discharged as a standing committee—with thanks.

Other Matters

Before the pastor arrives, the committee needs to be sure that the following concerns are passed on to the appropriate persons, committees, and boards to be handled.

1. The chairperson of the church or the board chairperson should communicate regularly with the pastor-elect. The pastor-elect should receive all bulletins, calendars, and important information during the interim.

2. If a parsonage is provided, it should be redecorated according to the taste of the pastor's family. Trustees should thoroughly inspect the entire building and make all necessary repairs. It goes without saying that stove, refrigerator, washer and dryer, large drapes, and carpeting are really fixed installations and should be provided by the church.

3. The study should be inspected carefully and all repairs and redecorating should be done before the pastor moves in.

4. In the event that the furniture arrives after the pastor and family have arrived (as is quite often the case), provision for living quarters should be made—at the church's expense.

5. If a house is to be purchased and the deal has not been consum-

mated or the house is not ready for occupancy, then the church should help the pastor find suitable quarters (usually at his or her expense) and give assistance to storing furniture until the housing is ready.

6. Provision should be made to greet the family as they arrive. Many town and country churches make a lovely gesture of concern by providing food items, through a kitchen shower, on the day the new pastor and family arrive.

The Installation

An installation is many things. For those churches of the free church tradition, in which the local church ordains, the service is a recognition of prior ordination. It is a solemn "rite of passage" and the beginning of a new chapter in the life of the church. The entire community publicly recognizes the installation as such. The service of installation is a covenanting service in which both pastor and people vow to work together for the ministry of the local church. Finally, it is a welcome of the pastor and his or her family to a large, new, extended family that is your church.

The life of the pastoral relations committee now takes on another role, that which has been described in the first two chapters. Upon its shoulders now lies the task of helping the new pastor begin well a long, happy, and fruitful ministry in the church. Let Paul's advice be characteristic of the pastoral relations committee's good ministry: "But we beseech you, brethren, to respect those who labor among you and are over you in the Lord and admonish you, and to esteem them very highly in love because of their work. Be at peace among yourselves" (1 Thessalonians 5:12-13).

Notes

Chapter 1

[1]Robert S. Paul, *Ministry* (Grand Rapids: Wm. B. Eerdmans Publishing Co., 1965), p. 59.

[2]James Allen Sparks, *Potshots at the Preacher* (Nashville: Abingdon Press, 1977), p. 9.

[3]Robert D. Rasmussen, "Pastoral Relations Committee" (Valley Forge: Commission on the Ministry, 1975), p. 3.

[4]*Ibid.*, pp. 13-15.

[5]*Ibid.*, p. 13.

[6]*Ibid.*, p. 15.

[7]Roy M. Oswald, *New Beginnings: Pastorate Start Up Workbook* (Washington, D.C.: The Alban Institute, Inc., 1977), p. 53.

[8]Rasmussen, "Pastoral Relations Committee," p. 15.

Chapter 2

[1]Edward W. Pierce, III, "Using the Pastoral Relations Committee as a Support System," *Minister* (Valley Forge: The Ministers Council), vol. 1, no. 3 (November, 1980), p. 5.

[2]Roy M. Oswald, *New Beginnings: Pastorate Start Up Workbook* (Washington, D.C.: The Alban Institute, Inc., 1977), pp. 49-50.

[3]Pierce, "Using the Pastoral Relations Committee," p. 5.

[4]*Ibid.* Pierce lists his system of using the problem-solving model on page 9.

1. Identifying and defining the problem.
2. Discovering the cause(s) and scope of the issue.
3. Developing strategy designs for solving the problem.

a. Resource person.
b. Bibliography.
4. Choosing and implementing strategy.
  a. Input and inclusion of the spouse.
5. Evaluation.
  a. ABPS profiles.
  b. Interview questionnaire.

[5] Oswald, *New Beginnings*, p. 1.

[6] Used in the first three chapters of Oswald's *New Beginnings*.

[7] G. Lloyd Rediger, "Let's Get the Pastor," *the christian Ministry* (March, 1978), p. 31.

[8] Speed B. Leas, *A Lay Person's Guide to Conflict Management* (Washington, D.C.: The Alban Institute, Inc., 1979) and Richard E. Rusbuldt, *Basic Leader Skills* (Valley Forge: Judson Press, 1981).

[9] Richard E. Rusbuldt, *Basic Leader Skills* (Valley Forge: Judson Press, 1981), p. 44.

[10] Speed Leas and Paul Kittlaus, *Church Fights* (Philadelphia: The Westminster Press, 1973), pp. 16-17.

[11] Rusbuldt, *Basic Leader Skills*, p. 47.

[12] *Ibid.*, p. 49.

[13] Rebecca E. Hight, "Burnout," *the christian Ministry* (July, 1980), p. 31.

[14] *Ibid.*

[15] *Ibid.*

[16] Oswald, *New Beginnings*, pp. 16-17.

[17] Wayne E. Oates, *Confessions of a Workaholic* (Nashville: Abingdon Press, 1971), p. 3.

[18] Beverly Croskery, "The Wife's View of Parish Life," *the christian Ministry* (January, 1977), pp. 10-11.

[19] Lyle E. Schaller, "Reviewing the Pastor's Contract," *the christian Ministry* (March, 1978), p. 19.

[20] Robert D. Rasmussen, "Pastoral Relations Committee," (Valley Forge: Commission on the Ministry, 1975), p. 9.

[21] Glenn and Margaret Ann Arnold, "Setting the Salary," *Moody Monthly* (January, 1974), pp. 42-43.

[22] Hugh O. Chambliss, "How Much Should a Church Pay Its Pastor?" *Church Administration* (March, 1973), p. 16.

[23] Lyle E. Schaller, *The Pastor and the People* (Nashville: Abingdon Press, 1973), pp. 73-74.

[24] Horace O. Duke, "Are You Ready for a Housing Allowance?" *Church Administration* (n.d.), p. 34.

[25] Chambliss, "How Much?" p. 39.

[26] Fredrick Herzberg, quoted by Richard J. Kirk, "On the Calling and Care of Pastors" (Washington, D.C.: The Alban Institute, Inc., 1980), pp. 8-10.

[27] *Ibid.*, p. 11.

[28] Mark Rouch, *Competent Ministry: A Guide to Effective Continuing Education* (Nashville: Abingdon Press, 1974), p. 23.

[29] *Ibid.*, p. 17.

[30] *Ibid.*, pp. 19-21.

[31] *Ibid.*, pp. 53-58.

[32] David C. Pohl, "Ministerial Sabbaticals," *the christian Ministry* (January, 1978), p. 8.
[33] Rasmussen, "Pastoral Relations Committee," p. 11.

Chapter 3

[1] Lyle E. Schaller, "The End of a Pastorate," *Parish Paper* (Richmond, Ind.: Yokefellows Institute, 1976).
[2] Gerald W. Gillaspie, *The Restless Pastor* (Chicago: Moody Press, 1974), pp. 40-45.
[3] Homer Carter, "The Grief in Leaving a Pastorate," *Church Administration* (March, 1973), p. 44.
[4] Celia A. Hahn, *The Minister Is Leaving* (New York: The Seabury Press, Inc., 1974), p. 96.
[5] Carter, "The Grief."
[6] Schaller, "The End."
[7] Hahn, *The Minister Is Leaving*, pp. 96-100.
[8] *Ibid.*, pp. 98-99.
[9] Roy M. Oswald, *Running Through the Thistles* (Washington, D.C.: The Alban Institute, Inc., 1978), pp. 10-11.
[10] *Ibid.*, p. 11.
[11] Schaller, "The End."
[12] *Ibid.*, pp. 11-12.
[13] Oswald, *Running*, pp. 6-7.
[14] Carter, "The Grief," p. 48.
[15] *Ibid.*
[16] Nancy Karo, *Adventure in Dying* (Chicago: Moody Press, 1976), pp. 213-214.
[17] Nancy Karo Johnson, *Alone and Beginning Again* (Valley Forge: Judson Press, 1982), pp. 52-53.

Chapter 4

[1] Philip Porcher, "What You Can Expect from an Interim Pastor and an Interim Consultant" (Washington, D.C.: The Alban Institute, Inc., 1980), p. 1.
[2] Leonard Hill, *Your Work on the Pulpit Committee* (Nashville: Broadman Press, 1970), pp. 21-22.
[3] Lyle E. Schaller, *The Pastor and the People* (Nashville: Abingdon Press, 1973), pp. 61-63.
[4] Fred Prinzing, "Filling the Gap," *Moody Monthly* (January, 1974), p. 40.
[5] *Ibid.*
[6] Porcher, "What You Can Expect," pp. 4-5.
[7] *Ibid.*, p. 4.

Chapter 5

[1] Garland A. Hendricks, *When a Church Is Seeking a Pastor* (Nashville: Sunday School Board of the Southern Baptist Convention, 1972), p. 5.
[2] Gerald M. Williamson, *Pastor Search Committee Primer* (Nashville: Broadman Press, 1981), pp. 9-10.

[3] Leonard Hill, *Your Work on the Pulpit Committee* (Nashville: Broadman Press, 1970), pp. 15-16.

[4] Ken McQuere, "Finding God's Man," *Moody Monthly* (January, 1974), p. 41.

[5] Lyle E. Schaller, *The Pastor and the People* (Nashville: Abingdon Press, 1973), pp. 46-47.

[6] *Ibid.*, p. 30.

[7] Robert R. Ebert, "The Professional Placement Service of the A.B.C. (An Economist's View)," *Freedom* (1982), p. 4.

Appendix A

Suggested Resources

The Art of Pastoral Conversation, Gaylord Noyce (Atlanta: John Knox Press, 1981).

The Authentic Pastor, Gene E. Bartlett (Valley Forge, Pa.: Judson Press, 1978).

Beginning a New Pastorate, Robert G. Kemper (Nashville: Abingdon Press, 1978).

Beyond Termination, Myra Marshal, with Dan McGee and Jennifer Owen (Nashville: Broadman Press, 1990).

The Care and Feeding of Volunteers, Douglas W. Johnson (Nashville: Abingdon Press, 1978).

Coping with Clergy Burnout, G. Lloyd Rediger (Valley Forge, Pa.: Judson Press, 1982).

Every Pastor Needs a Pastor, Louis McBurney (Waco: Word, Inc., 1977).

The Gift of Administration, Thomas C. Campbell and Gary B. Reierson (Philadelphia: The Westminster Press, 1981).

Hidden World of the Pastor, Kenneth L. Swetland (Grand Rapids: Baker Books, 1995).

A Layperson's Guide to Conflict Management, Speed B. Leas (Washington, D.C.: The Alban Institute, Inc., 1979).

Managing Stress in Ministry, William E. Hume (San Francisco: Harper and Row, 1985).

The Mid-life Crisis of a Minister, Ray G. Ragsdale (Waco: Word, Inc., 1978).

New Beginnings: Pastorate Start Up Workbook, Roy M. Oswald (Washington, D.C.: The Alban Institute, 1977).

The Pastor and the People, Lyle E. Schaller (Nashville: Abingdon Press, 1973).

Pastor Preacher Person, David K. Switzer (Nashville: Abingdon Press, 1979).

Pastoral Stress, Anthony G. Pappas (Alban Institute, 1995).

Person and Profession, Charles W. Stewart (Nashville: Abingdon Press, 1974).

The Positive Use of the Minister's Role, David C. Jacobsen (Philadelphia: The Westminster Press, 1967).

Support Your Local Pastor, Wes Roberts (Colorado Springs: Nav Press, 1995).

There's Algae in the Baptismal 'Fount,' Daniel Zeluff (Nashville: Abingdon Press, 1978).

Time Management, Speed B. Leas (Nashville: Abingdon Press, 1978).

The Time of Your Life: Self/Time Management for Pastors, Robert L. Randall (Nashville: Abingdon Press, 1994).

"Today's Congregation in Today's World Needs a Pastor Who Continually Grows," brochure available from The Society for the Advancement of Continuing Education for Ministry, 855 Locust Street, Collegeville, PA 19426.

The following books relate to clergy sexual misconduct

Betrayal of Trust, Sexual Misconduct in the Pastorate, Stanley J. Grenz and Roy D. Bell (Downers Grove, Il.: InterVarsity Press, 1995).

Ethics in Pastoral Ministry, Richard M. Gula (New York: Paulist Press, 1996).

Ministry and Sexuality, G. Lloyd Rediger (Minneapolis: Fortress Press, 1990).

Sexual Abuse by Clergy: A Crisis for the Church, Maria M. Fortune and James N. Poling (Decatur, Ga.: Journal of Pastoral Care Publications, Inc., 1994).

When a Leader Falls, What Happens to Everyone Else? Jan Winebrenner and Debra Frazer (Minneapolis: Bethany House Publishers, 1993).

When Ministers Sin: Sexual Abuse in the Churches, Neil and Thea Omerod (Australia: Millennium Books, 1995).

Appendix B

The Annual Review of the Pastor-Church Relationship*

The courtship is through, the marriage vows have been said; now the honeymoon starts. During this period the church is happy. The sermons are fresh and relevant. New programs are inaugurated and all is well.

After six months inherent flaws in both partners of this marriage often begin to show up. People begin to realize that the pastor is not perfect and the pastor may be disappointed in people or programs.

Give the marriage a chance. The words "for better or for worse" have some transfer of meaning here. In marriages that last, the partners learn to accept the failings and the flaws of the other. When the failings show up—as they surely will—mature people do not give up and do not ask for divorce. To be sure, on rare occasions the realization that a mismatch has occurred is seen and the pastor leaves.

The relationship of pastor and people is unique upon the face of the earth. To make it go, both have to work at it and accept what the other brings to the union.

Human frailties are there but usually are not insurmountable. This is why it was so important back in the negotiating stages to provide for a six-month review so that, as the people of God, the pastor and people can openly and honestly talk over problems.

It is also important that there be an ongoing process of evaluation.

*Adapted from Ministerial Guidance Committee, "How to Treat Your Pastor" (St. Paul: Minnesota Baptist Conference, 1976), pp. 7-14. This review was prepared by John Wiens and used by permission of the Christian Century Foundation.

An annual review, using the following document as the instrument for evaluating, is helpful.

This instrument is designed to assist the pastoral relations committee of the local church in its annual review of the relationship between the pastor and the congregation. Most churches and pastors recognize the value of such an annual review. Many church constitutions require it. Yet too often the discussions have only limited effectiveness, being given largely to generalities. The most specific matter is usually the pastor's salary, but all too often that is considered independently instead of in relation to the pastor's total performance. Unfortunately, there are times when this annual meeting has been restricted to a discussion of one or two "pet gripes."

It is intended that this form give comprehensiveness to the annual review. *It is for use by the pastoral relations committee only, not the entire congregation.* Copies may be given to the members of the committee in advance of the meeting in order that all of the time together may be spent in discussion. The forms should be discarded once the review has been completed.

The exact score recorded by committee members is not important. Indeed, there are categories on which some will plead complete ignorance. Yet even these can be important in creating a needed awareness. The aim is to bring into open discussion the perception the pastor and the congregation have of the performance of the other and also the expectation each has of the other. Indeed, it is to share openly all pertinent concerns, to discover and affirm strengths, and to discover and help with weaknesses. It is to bring into the open any existing differences, in order that they might be understood, and with Christian spirit, either resolved or creatively dealt with in a manner considerate of both the pastor and the congregation. In summary, the aim is mutual awareness and open discussion, leading to greater understanding and partnership in Christian service.

I. The Pastor's Time
(to be filled out by all committee members, including the pastor)

It is recognized that many responses will be approximations. Nonetheless, it is usually more helpful to discuss a given concern even on that basis rather than to maintain silence.

Lay members should rate not only their own ideas, impressions, or perceptions, but also, as much as possible, the congregation's thoughts. The discussion which follows, based on a comparison of what committee members recorded, should highlight areas in which the pastor, unknown to the other members or the congregation, has had to spend considerable time. Also, it should highlight differences which might exist among members or between the congregation and the pastor on the amount of time he or she gives or does not give to a given area.

In most categories you will be asked to register your response on a scale of one to five, the one standing for low or dissatisfied, the five for high or satisfied. Checking a category as four might mean that although you are generally satisfied, there is one area of that particular category in which you would like to see some change.

A. The Pastor's Use of His or Her Time

   1. Soul and mind stretching through personal study/prayer/reflection

      Low __ __ __ __ __ High
          1   2   3   4   5

   2. Fellowship with his or her family

      Low __ __ __ __ __ High
          1   2   3   4   5

   3. Within the church

      a. Sermon study and preparation

         Low __ __ __ __ __ High
             1   2   3   4   5

      b. Administration

         Low __ __ __ __ __ High
             1   2   3   4   5

      c. Teaching/equipping

         Low __ __ __ __ __ High
             1   2   3   4   5

d. Pastoral care

   (1) Building relationships with congregation

                               Low __ __ __ __ __ High
                                       1 2 3 4 5

   (2) Counseling

                               Low __ __ __ __ __ High
                                       1 2 3 4 5

   (3) Visitation

      (a) Prospective members

                               Low __ __ __ __ __ High
                                     1 2 3 4 5

      (b) Sick

                               Low __ __ __ __ __ High
                                     1 2 3 4 5

      (c) General members

                               Low __ __ __ __ __ High
                                     1 2 3 4 5

      (d) Crisis situations

                               Low __ __ __ __ __ High
                                     1 2 3 4 5

4. Evangelism

                               Low __ __ __ __ __ High
                                     1 2 3 4 5

5. Fellowship/study/support building with other ministers

                               Low __ __ __ __ __ High
                                     1 2 3 4 5

6. Formal continuing education

                               Low __ __ __ __ __ High
                                     1 2 3 4 5

7. Denominational

Low __ __ __ __ __ High
     1   2   3   4   5

8. Ecumenical/community

Low __ __ __ __ __ High
     1   2   3   4   5

B. Hours per Week Expected of the Pastor

Please circle your (or the congregation's) expectation; then underline the hours you think the pastor puts in per week.

30—35   40—45   50—55   60—65
35—40   45—50   55—60   65—70

( )   Including time spent in ministry for your denomination and community

( )   Excluding time spent in ministry for your denomination and community

II. The Church's Support of Its Pastor
(to be filled out by all committee members, including the pastor)

A. This church clearly defines the competencies it expects of its pastor.

Low __ __ __ __ __ High
     1   2   3   4   5

B. This church understands and accepts the role of the pastor in a way consistent with the pastor's self-understanding, abilities, and strengths.

Low __ __ __ __ __ High
     1   2   3   4   5

C. This church provides resources necessary for the ministry and program it is expecting its pastor to fulfill and carry out.

Low __ __ __ __ __ High
     1   2   3   4   5

D. This church provides follow-through support for decisions made by the congregation, matching the commitment it is expecting from the pastor.

Low __ __ __ __ __ High
     1   2   3   4   5

E. This church allows the pastor to be human (limited and possessing weaknesses as well as strengths).

Low __ __ __ __ __ High
     1   2   3   4   5

F. This church allows the pastor to be himself or herself (does not try to make him or her someone else).

Low__ __ __ __ __ High
     1   2   3   4   5

G. This church is supportive and remedial in its response and criticism, rather than blaming.

Low __ __ __ __ __ High
     1   2   3   4   5

III. The Exercise of Authority in This Congregation
(to be filled out by all committee members, including the pastor)

In many things each congregation has its own style, and to a degree this is good. Periodic self-evaluation and exploration of better patterns of decision making must, however, be included in the rhythm of healthy corporate life. Included are questions such as these: How is authority exercised in our congregation? How are decisions made and implemented? How is direction determined?

	Yes	No	Some-what
A. "According to constitution" (undue emphasis upon everything being "prim and proper")	____	____	____
B. Authoritarian (expecting others to follow without giving them a voice)	____	____	____
C. Through unofficial powerful persons	____	____	____

D. By decision of a representative group   ____   ____   ____

E. "Herr Pastor" aloofness (impersonal and distant)   ____   ____   ____

F. Through proper delegation, equipping, and encouragement of others   ____   ____   ____

G. By the pastor doing the work rather than equipping and delegating   ____   ____   ____

H. By building relations   ____   ____   ____

I. With rigid adherence to tradition   ____   ____   ____

J. With discriminating openness to change   ____   ____   ____

K. By moving with fashion fad   ____   ____   ____

L. By free and open sharing of information, ideas, and possibilities   ____   ____   ____

M. By encouraging an honest and open facing of problems   ____   ____   ____

N. By being sensitive to both facts and feelings   ____   ____   ____

O. With collegiality in staff relationships   ____   ____   ____

IV. Effectiveness Evaluator
(to be filled out by laypersons on the pastoral relations committee)

A. There is a workable affinity between the goals of the pastor and the goals of the congregation.

Low __ __ __ __ __ High
     1   2   3   4   5

B. The pastor is sensitive to/aware of the needs of the congregation.

Low __ __ __ __ __ High
     1   2   3   4   5

C. The pastor is a good listener.

Low __ __ __ __ __ High
    1 2 3 4 5

D. The pastor encourages and personally models a mutual Christian caring.

Low __ __ __ __ __ High
    1 2 3 4 5

E. The trust level between the pastor and the congregation is of sufficient depth and breadth to constitute an effective partnership.

Low __ __ __ __ __ High
    1 2 3 4 5

F. The pastor includes in his or her perspective the goals of the congregation as a whole, and does not restrict his or her work to the goals of one segment.

Low __ __ __ __ __ High
    1 2 3 4 5

G. The pastor is able to communicate effectively in preaching.

Low __ __ __ __ __ High
    1 2 3 4 5

H. The pastor is an effective worship leader.

Low __ __ __ __ __ High
    1 2 3 4 5

I. The pastor has a good pulpit decorum.

Low __ __ __ __ __ High
    1 2 3 4 5

J. The pastor fits the congregation's image of a pastor.

Low __ __ __ __ __ High
    1 2 3 4 5

V. The Pastor's Material Needs

	Adequate	Tolerable/ Acceptable	Inadequate
A. Salary	——	——	——
B. Housing	——	——	——
C. Medical Insurance	——	——	——
D. Car Allowance	——	——	——
E. Denominational Conferences	——	——	——
F. Continuing Education and Other Professional Expenses	——	——	——
G. Vacation Time	——	——	——
H. Pension and Retirement Program	——	——	——

Appendix C

What to Leave

It is not expected that the departing pastor so order church affairs that an agenda is written for the new pastor. The departing pastor should let that person know what has been going on. The following checklist may be helpful.

1. Leave and *label* all keys.

2. Provide for the trustees a list of all repairs or changes that need to be made in the parsonage, study, and church building.

3. Provide a list of how to work things and who-to-call-if. Names of immediate neighbors will be helpful.

4. Leave a complete record of funerals and weddings you have conducted. Dates of weddings and the maiden names involved will help the new pastor to be oriented to the congregation. Recent bereavements especially will be important for your successor to know about.

5. A complete and up-to-date membership record should be left. While this is the task of the church clerk, it is the pastor's duty to ask that it be done.

6. Sunday church school records are notoriously poor in most churches. For outreach purposes alone, the pastor needs a good record of Sunday church school families. The same is true for boys' and girls' clubs within the church.

7. A list of prospects you have been working on is important. Make the list as complete as possible, with annotations that would be helpful for the new pastor as he or she begins calling.

8. Bound copies of church bulletins and/or church papers are immeasurably helpful for your successor's orientation.

9. The most important item for the beginning of a ministry is a set of 3″ x 5″ cards with names of church members, their occupations (including where they work), family relationships, and positions held within the church. It will serve no useful purpose to note that Mr. X has been nothing but a troublemaker or that Mrs. Y is not active! Let the new pastor learn that. And perhaps he or she will be able to challenge those persons in ways you were unable to. Leave the list black and white. Don't color the names in!

10. A list of suppliers for various items the church purchases is a must. A list of emergency repair persons is also important.

11. An annual calendar of church dates will be helpful. The dates are subject to change by your successor, but he or she needs to know what course has been set.

12. A roster of current church officers (with addresses and names) plus a listing of all committee personnel and volunteer leaders of all kinds are necessary.

13. Constitutions and manuals of operation are all helpful to an understanding of church operations, but a list of "church traditions" is invaluable to orienting the pastor to the new charges. The knowledge, for instance, that the church has strong Swedish roots and has conducted a Swedish "Julotta" service at 6 A.M. every Christmas for the last eighty-nine years is something the pastor needs! Without indicating that they must be continued, an explanation of the traditions of the church up to now will be welcomed by the new minister.

14. Leave a good name. Nothing you can do in the last days of your pastorate can make a good name for you if you haven't lived a gracious Christian life up until now. But leaving bills unpaid (or without at least an understanding that they will be paid) only leaves a bad name for you and casts reflection on the ministry and on the church of Jesus Christ.

Appendix D*

Letter to the Congregation from the Chairperson

(could be printed in church calendar and/or mailed to the members)

Dear Friends:

Our church has entrusted five of your fellow members with the task of seeking a successor to our pastor, the Reverend Paul Apostle, who resigned on September 25. We know you will remember us prayerfully as we go about this in a responsible manner.

It may be helpful to you if we share some information about the accepted procedures by which pulpit committees operate.

1. It is the committee's job to seek complete information regarding all those whose names are received, either from a seminary, denominational office or from other reliable sources.

2. We shall select, after prayer and mutual counsel, those few people who seem to us to be most promising; we shall write or call them to determine their possible interest, hear them in their pulpits, and then decide upon the one we wish to recommend for our congregational consideration and vote.

3. We shall not present to our church more than one candidate at any time, and that only after we have given the members full information regarding him/her.

It is our prayerful hope that the Lord may lead us to make a unanimous recommendation.

*Portions of Appendixes D, E, F, G, H, I, J, K, and L are adapted from *Procedures in Calling a Pastor*, by Emmett V. Johnson, pp. 51-58, 62-66, 74-78.

Please remember that the experience of our churches shows that the search for a new pastor requires time—months, possibly a year or more. We need your patience and confidence. It is not possible for us to tell anyone whom we are considering, lest the prospective candidate be embarrassed and withdraw his or her name from consideration.

We shall be absent on certain Sundays, hearing recommended persons, but do not ask us where we are going or whom we have heard.

During this time we will have interim or guest ministers. We have agreed with them that their names shall not be considered as candidates.

We are enclosing a questionnaire that will help us in our work. Please fill it out and bring it to church.

Please understand that when we are ready to make a recommendation, all church members will be given the most complete information and will be given it at the same time. Thank you for the trust that you have placed in us, and do not forget to remember us in your prayers.

Sincerely,

Lars E. Larson, *Chairperson*
Enclosure

Appendix E

The Church Profile

History

Brief summary of origin and development of church.
Factors in the past that affected growth and development.
General description of the work of former pastors, their length of service.

Statistics

Size of present membership, including number who are nonresident or inactive; chart showing growth or decline of membership during past twenty years.
Number of additions by baptism and church letter.
Enrollment and average attendance at meetings of all church organizations; comparison with figures for past several years.
Average attendance at worship services now and comparison with past several years.
Amount of church budget with items listed in detail.
Financial report showing actual income and expenditures, including total gifts for missions (show breakdown of mission giving).
Amount of church debt and how it is financed.
Increase or decrease of attendance and offerings during last few years.

Physical Property

Size and arrangement of buildings and parking area.
Property limitations and possibilities for future expansion.
Description of parsonage.

Organizations and Objectives

List and description of all church organizations, committees, and so
on, with explanation of how they are financed, staffed, and related
to one another.

Description of weekday programs and special projects.

List of paid church staff, including job descriptions and relationship
to pastor.

Comparison of number of volunteer workers to number of jobs to be
filled.

Church calendar, including long-range plans adopted or under consideration.

Description of Membership

Size and special needs of various age groups.

Occupations, education, income, and interests of members.

Description of Community

Population: whether growing, declining, or static.

Rural or urban: downtown or residential or in transition.

Ethnic groups.

Sources of income of people.

Cost of living.

Schools, hospitals, and other institutions.

Other Baptist churches; churches of other denominations.

Extent of territory from which church draws members—with map
indicating location of member families in relation to church.

Anticipated changes: business expected to move in or out, expand
or decline; new highways in area; urban renewal plans.

Special problems or opportunities in community.

Attitudes of Church Members

Interest in evangelism, missions, stewardship, and social ministry.

Outlook on building expansion, expansion of church staff, or church
organizations.

Willingness to cooperate with the pastor.

Outlook on cooperating with other churches in the community.

Attitudes toward ministering to all races and meeting community needs.

Factors tending to weaken or strengthen the unity and fellowship of the church.

Whether progressive in spirit or slow to accept changes.

Customs peculiar to the church or community.

Realistic appraisal of freedom and restrictions of office of pastor.

Appendix F

The Congregational Questionnaire

To Members and Friends of First Baptist Church:

What qualities do you consider to be important in the next pastor of First Baptist?

What direction do you think the total program of the church should take?

The pulpit committee is eager to know how you feel about these questions. If you will carefully answer the following questions, giving your opinion, you will help us in our effort to find the one who should lead our congregation in the years ahead.

Please number in order of importance (1-8, 1 being the most important) what you consider to be the most important qualities in a prospective pastor. (Naturally we all consider *all* of them important, but what do you consider *most* important?)

___ Preaching ability

___ Worker with young people

___ Enthusiasm for visitation

___ Administrative and organizational ability

___ Personal evangelism

___ Willingness and ability to give personal counsel

___ Warm, friendly personality

___ Other (please specify)

Would you like First Baptist to have more or less emphasis on the following?

Write "more" for "I would like greater emphasis."

Write "less" for "less emphasis, please."

Write "same" for "about the same as now."

___ Expository Bible preaching

___ Evangelistic preaching

___ Personal evangelism

___ Group prayer

___ Social action

___ Young people's activities

___ Foreign and home missions

___ Fellowship activities

___ Group Bible study

___ Other (please specify)

Please check the blanks below that describe *you*. (No names, please, unless you desire to be identified.)

___ Member   ___ Male   Age: ___ Over 50

___ Nonmember   ___ Female   ___ 35 to 50

                                           ___ 20 to 35

                                           ___ 15 to 20

                                           ___ Under 15

If you have an age preference for a pastor, please check:

         ___ 25 to 35   ___ 35 to 45   ___ Over 45

Appendix G

A Pastor's Priorities

Visiting Calling in the homes of members or at their places of work in a systematic program to meet each member on his or her own turf.	*Community Leader* Serving as a volunteer leader in the community to help make this a better world for all God's children.
Teaching Teaching the instruction class, planning and/or teaching classes for church school teachers, teaching in special short-term classes, and so on.	*The Leader* Serving as *the* leader in the congregation—the person to whom members turn for advice and guidance on all aspects of the life and work of the congregation.
Counseling Counseling with individuals on personal and spiritual problems, with couples planning to be married, with those who are hospitalized, with other people on personal and vocational problems, and so on.	*Personal and Spiritual Growth* Developing and following a discipline of Bible and other devotional study, participating in programs of continuing education, and helping to plan and lead opportunities for personal and spiritual growth for others.

Administration Serving as "executive secretary" of the congregation, working with committees, helping to plan the financial program of the church, working with committees on planning and implementing programs, and so on.	*Denominational Responsibilities* Carrying a fair share of denominational responsibilities, participating in other cooperative bodies. Also enlisting denominational and other resources for use in the local situation.
Evangelism Calling on the unchurched people in the community, bearing witness to the Good News, calling on prospective new members, and training laypersons to be evangelists.	*Leading Worship and Preaching* Planning and conducting worship services, including sermon preparation and working with others who will participate in leading corporate worship.
A Leader Among Leaders Serving with the lay leadership as one of the core of leaders in the congregation—each with his or her own special responsibilities and each with his or her own unique gifts.	*Enabler* Helping others identify their own special call to service and ministry and enabling them to respond to that call.

What Are the Priorities?

What are the priorities on the minister's time in your congregation? What does the minister see as the order of priority on his or her time? What do the members believe it to be?

One way to find the answers to these and related questions in your parish is to use a set of cards similar to those shown under "A Pastor's Priorities." Here is a suggested procedure for using this process.

1. Reproduce enough copies so that each member of the committee will have one sheet listing the priorities on the pastor's time in your parish.

2. Cut the sheets so that each person has one set of cards; distribute one pack of cards to each person around a table.

3. Clarify the ground rules. Is the question to be answered "What *are* the priorities on the pastor's time in this congregation?" or "What *should* be the priorities?" or something else? Make sure everyone is responding to the same question.

4. Give everyone from five to ten minutes to look at the cards and sort them out, discarding what he or she believes to be the four *lowest* priorities on the pastor's time or the least important functions. *Without discussing what they are doing or the reasons for their choices,* each person should arrange the remaining cards in the order of importance.

5. Begin with one of the laypersons and, moving in rotation around the table, ask each person to lay down the top priority card, face up on the table. While doing this, let each person state what he or she has chosen as the top priority and why. Continue around the table until everyone has placed a top priority card on the table. (It is often helpful if the minister is the last to show his or her card.)

6. Discuss what the cards reveal. Are they all the same? Are there differences? If so, what do the differences suggest?

7. Continue the same pattern, with each person laying his or her second priority card just below the one placed on the table earlier. Discuss what the trend appears to be.

8. Continue with six more rounds.

9. Look at the four cards each person discarded earlier. Is there anything resembling a consensus in the discards?

Use this in any way you wish as a tool to stimulate creative and constructive discussion. Have fun!

(Adapted and used by permission of Lyle Schaller)

Appendix H

Guidelines for Telephone Interview with a Reference Person

Date _____

Name of potential candidate _____

Reference person contacted _____

    Phone: Home _____

           Office _____

Mr./Mrs./Miss _____, this is _____ with First Baptist Church in Andover, Minnesota. We are in search of a pastor, and a person you are acquainted with, _____, is being considered for this position. Your name has been suggested/given by _____ as a reference. Information you relate to me will be kept within our pastoral search committee.

I. Background Information on Reference

1. What is/was the nature of your work? _____

2. What is/was the nature of his or her work? _____

3. What church was this person serving as related to this reference?

   _____

4. What is/was your position in the church, seminary, and so on, in relationship to that of _____? _____

5. What church is he or she presently serving? _____

   And in what city is it located? _____

6. How long have you known _____? _____

   II. Administrative Qualities, Style, and Effectiveness

7. How effective as an administrator would you consider him or her to be?

   _____

8. Would you say that his or her administrative style is autocratic, rather forceful, or democratic in nature?

   Autocratic-forceful ____
   Democratic _____

   III. Candidate's Spiritual Qualities and Practice

9. Would you consider _____ a student of the Word? __

10. What do you know about his or her Bible study habits? _____

11. What do you know about his or her prayer life? _____

12. In his or her spiritual life, would you consider him or her to have a warm, loving spirit? _____

13. Does his or her personality display humility and forgiveness? __

   IV. Candidate's Self-Discipline

14. Is he or she able to organize himself or herself and his or her work?

   _____

15. Is he or she goal-oriented? _____

16. Would you consider him or her energetic and industrious? _____

   V. Preaching Ability and Style

17. Would you consider him or her to be a biblical preacher?

   _____

18. On a scale of 1-10, how effective was/is _____ in his or her preaching and teaching ministry? Content _____ Delivery _____

19. Do you know much about his or her counseling ministry? _____ Does he or she like to counsel people? _____ Do you know how effective he or she is in his or her counseling ministry? _____

VI. Church Programming and Implementation

20. With what denomination is his or her present church associated?

_____

21. What do you know about the growth of the church during his or her years as _____? Membership? _____ Morning service attendance? _____ What contribution did he or she make in his or her capacity as _____ to this growth? _____

22. Do you know any church budget figures?: General _____ Missions _____

23. Is he or she able to initiate programs, get people to accept these programs, and organize people to implement these programs?

_____

24. What emphasis does he or she place on missions? _____

25. Does he or she present new and creative programs to the church?

_____

26. Would you say that most of his or her programs are/have been effective?

_____

VII. Relationship with People and Ability to Motivate

27. Is he or she able to motivate people? _____

28. Does he or she have any personality traits or life-style habits that adversely affect the board members or church members? _____

_____

29. How would you rate him or her in getting along with others? Excellent _____ Very good _____ Fair _____

30. In your opinion, is there any reason he or she should want to leave his or her present position? _____

31. In your estimation, does he or she have a good family life? _____

VIII. Candidate's Strengths and Weaknesses

32. What would you say are some of his or her strong points? _____

_____

_____

_____

33. What would you say are some of his or her weak points? _____

_____

_____

_____

34. From your experience with _____, what would you say
    could be done to help him or her become more effective? _____

_____

35. Do you know any other person that knows _____ that
    we could contact as a reference? _____

            Person who called this reference _____
                                             Signature

Appendix I*

Letter to Candidate

Dear Pastor Peterson:

Our pastor, the Reverend Paul Apostle, has resigned to become pastor of First Baptist Church, Minneapolis. A pulpit committee has been formed to seek and recommend a successor. It is with this concern that I write to you.

Enclosed are two items which will give you insight into our ministry: our church constitution and a profile of our church and parsonage.

Your name has been made known to us as someone who would give outstanding leadership to our church. We are therefore interested in visiting with you.

Without any commitment on your part or that of the church, we would like to know whether you would consider becoming our pastor should later contacts and conferences lead to a mutual interest.

If your answer is affirmative, we will arrange to visit you at your church on a mutually agreeable date.

We would be glad to receive your answer in the next two weeks. In the meantime, should you have any questions, please call me collect at _____, and I will be happy to give you further information. Whatever exchanges we have will be confidential.

Sincerely,

Lars E. Larson, *Chairperson, Pulpit Committee*

Enclosures (2)

*Appendices I and K are adapted from *Calling a Baptist Minister* (Valley Forge: Commission on the Ministry, American Baptist Churches in the U.S.A., 1974), pp. 44, 46-47. Appendices J and L are from pages 45, 49-52 of the same source.

P.S. If you are interested, contact us by return mail and include directions to your church, the time of your morning worship and any dates you will *not* be in the pulpit.

Appendix J

Suggested Outline of Letter to the Congregation

Announcing the Coming of a Candidate

(Date) _____

Dear Members of _____ Church:

    Indicate that at last you have good news for the church. After a long and careful search you are ready to present a name to the church as a candidate for pastor. Note that enclosed in the letter is a biographical summary of the Rev. (_____) of (_____), (_____), who is being recommended by the pulpit committee.

Paragraph #2—

    Report that the candidate (and spouse) has (have) visited your community, seen the church building and parsonage and, if the congregation is led to extend a call, the invitation will be given full consideration.

Paragraph #3—

    Say what arrangements have been made for the candidate to be presented to the church. If it is to be at a Sunday worship service or midweek service, indicate the date and time. Note whatever compliance with the bylaws is appropriate. State clearly when and under what circumstances the vote on whether or not to extend a call will be taken.

Paragraph #4—

Announce any additional opportunities that have been planned for the congregation to meet the candidate (and family), stating clearly the date, time, place, and nature of the occasion. Close the letter with a statement of the hope the committee has for the future of your church. Invite the prayerful support of the members of the church as they come to the time of decision.

Sincerely,

_____, Chairperson

Appendix K

Suggested Letter to Pastor-Elect

(Date) _____

Dear _____:

It is my pleasure to inform you that, by the vote of our congregation on (day, date, year), the (name of church) of (town of church) extends to you a unanimous call to become its pastor. The enthusiastic spirit of our people in accepting the pulpit committee's recommendation was a joy to us as we hope it will be to you.

The terms of the call, as agreed upon in your conference with our Pulpit Committee, are as follows:

The Church agrees:

(List terms)

You, as Pastor-Elect, agree:

1. To accept the pastoral leadership of the _____ Church of _____, beginning your ministry (month, date, year).

2. To assume responsibility for your participation as a self-employed person in Social Security.

3. To accept the provision in the bylaws of the _____ Church

of _____, whereby the pastoral relationship may be terminated by either pastor or church upon giving of a _____ day notice or by such notice as may be mutually agreed upon by both parties.

We have endeavored to outline as carefully and completely as possible, for your assurance and that of the church, the arrangements implicit in this call, and we shall appreciate having your written acceptance at the earliest possible date.

May God guide and bless both pastor-elect and people as we anticipate this forthcoming fellowship in Christian service.

By order of the church.

(Signed)

_____ Church Clerk

Appendix L

A Suggested Service of Installation

Prelude

Call to Worship

Hymn

Invocation and Lord's Prayer

Scripture Reading

Anthem or Solo

Sermon

Commitment of the Minister
and the Congregation

Charge to the Minister

_____ __ _____, having been ordained as a minister of Jesus Christ, and having accepted the invitation of the _____ Church of _____ to become its pastor, do you solemnly pledge that you will serve this congregation to the best of your ability, according to the affirmations you have given in your ordination?

Minister: I do.

Charge to the Minister

I charge you to be a good minister of Jesus Christ, remembering that like our Lord, you have come ''not to be served but to serve,'' and to keep yourself at all times in true devotion to your high calling. Will you seek to practice daily the faith you profess, administer the ordinances in purity, proclaim the truth with love, and endeavor to lead this people in the ways of Christ the Lord?

Minister: I will, God being my helper.

Charge to the Congregation

Are you persuaded as a church of Jesus Christ that you are ready to be instructed, led, and strengthened in the ways of the Spirit by the one who stands before you in answer to the call of God?

Congregation: We are.

Charge to the Congregation

In recognition of the Christian partnership that must exist between pastor and people, do you now affirm your loyalty to this church and to this pastoral relationship? Do you promise to give your utmost in devoted service and loyal cooperation?

Congregation: We do, God being our helper.

Prayer of Dedication

DECLARATION (By the church moderator or other presiding officer)

In the name of our Lord Jesus Christ, the head of the Church, we do declare you, _____ __ _____, to be installed as the pastor of this congregation of the _____ Church of _____. We shall pray for you and uphold you in all your duties as a minister of the gospel and, in token whereof, we now extend

to you the right hand of fellowship. The grace of our Lord Jesus Christ
be with you always and upon us all.

Amen.

Hymn

Benediction

Postlude

Further Suggestions

The minister (and family) will be ushered, by the chairman of the
deacons, to a pew at the front of the church where they will remain
until the minister goes to the platform or chancel for the Charge to the
Minister.

The moderator, the chairman of the pulpit committee, or some duly
appointed officer, should preside at the service.

Usually it is the custom to invite some representative of the region,
state, city society, or the denomination-at-large to participate in portions
of the service, such as the sermon, Charge to the Minister, Charge to
the Congregation, or Prayer of Dedication.

Because of the vital importance of a service of installation, it should
be held on a Sunday morning, when the largest possible participation
by the membership is expected. It is recommended that the ''welcome''
or ''reception'' with sister churches, when the general public is invited,
should be held separately, perhaps on a Sunday afternoon or on a week
night.

Following are suggestions for the service:

Special Music

Send Out Thy Light
Lord, Make Me an Instrument of Thy Peace
How Beautiful upon the Mountains
Thou Wilt Keep Him in Perfect Peace

The Lord's Prayer
How Lovely Are Thy Messengers
I Will Magnify Thee, O Lord

Scripture Readings

Matthew 23:1-12	1 Timothy 6:1-21
John 13:1-17	2 Timothy 1:1-18
Ephesians 4:1-16	2 Timothy 4:1-18
1 Peter 5:1-11	

Suggested Hymns

Lead On, O King Eternal
The Church's One Foundation
Guide Me, O Thou Great Jehovah
O Jesus, I Have Promised
O Master, Let Me Walk with Thee
Breathe on Me, Breath of God
O Zion, Haste
Blest Be the Tie